GoWise USA Air Fryer Cookbook

Legal

DISCLAIMER: This book is independently published by, and is **not** affiliated with, sponsored by, or endorsed by any of the products mentioned in this book. All other company and product names are the trademarks of their respective owners.

This information contained in this book is for entertainment purposes only. The content represents the opinion of the author and is based on the author's personal experience and observations. The author does not assume any liability whatsoever for the use of or inability to use any or all information contained in this book, and accepts no responsibility for any loss or damages of any kind that may be incurred by the reader as a result of actions arising from the use of the information in this book. Use this information at your own risk. No part of this book may be reproduced or transmitted in any form or by any means, electronic or mechanical, including photocopying, recording, or by any information storage or retrieval system, without express written permission from the author, except in the case of brief quotations embodied in critical articles and reviews – or except by a reviewer who may quote brief passages in a review.

Respective authors hold all copyrights not held by the publisher

---

NOTE: Some of the recipes in this book include raw eggs. Raw eggs may contain bacteria. It is recommended that you purchase certified salmonella-free eggs from a reliable source and store them in the refrigerator. You should not feed raw eggs to babies or small kids. Likewise, pregnant women, elderly persons, or those with a compromised immune system should not eat raw eggs. Neither the author nor the publisher claims responsibility for adverse effects resulting from the use of the recipes and/or information found within this book.

The author reserves the right to make any changes he or she deems necessary to future versions of the publication to ensure its accuracy.

COPYRIGHT © 2018, All Rights Reserved.

Published in The United States of America

Sarah Conner

Introduction

These air fryer recipes are a great asset to have as a part of your recipe playbook in preparing food in your kitchen. We've made it easy to follow and great to eat! We understand that everyone has lives and such a busy schedule that lots of families don't even have time to cook anymore. That's why this book is a must have for your kitchen.

We've "Packed a Punch" by adding these hand selected menu items for your devouring needs. Just imagine, coming home from work and not having time to cook being a "thing-of-the-past!" Just putting in the food and turning on the machine.

We've found that there are specific settings within the air fryer controls that make this device easy for anyone to cook up something delicious. Most of these recipes inside of this book are very healthy indeed! We always want to keep in account that there are a lot of families that want to eat as clean as they can and healthy.

We've also included some "mouth-watering" marinades that will make the juices of the meat you are preparing, melt in your mouth.

If you have kids then get them involved in this new revolutionary cooking process. It's as easy as 1 – 2 – 3!

GoWise USA Air Fryer Cookbook

Table of Contents

LEGAL	2
INTRODUCTION	3
TABLE OF CONTENTS	4
GOWISE OR GO HOME!!!	8
What We've Found That the GoWise Air Fryer Gives You	8
FEATURES	10
The Various Parts of Your Air Fryer	10
HOW TO USE	11
The Steps to Making Food in Your Air Fryer	11
CLEANING IS A BREEZE	12
How to Make Sure Your Air Fryer Stays Clean	12
COOKING TIPS	13
How to Optimize the Use of Your Air Fryer	13
LET THE COOKING BEGIN!	14
CHICKEN	15
Chicken Parma	16
Honey Sriracha Hot Wings	17
Tandoori Chicken	18
Parmesan Garlic Chicken Wings	20
Parmesan Garlic Chicken Tenders	21
Pizza Stuffed Chicken Thighs	22
Thai Chicken Eggrolls	23
Chicken Nuggets	25
Roast Chicken	26
Classic Fried Chicken Thighs	27
Nashville Hot Fried Chicken	28
Honey Garlic Chicken Wings	30
Crispy Restaurant Style Chicken Sandwiches	31
BBQ Chicken	33
Spicy BBQ Chicken	34
Crispy Chicken Breast	35

CRISPY SPICY CHICKEN BREAST	36
JERK CHICKEN WINGS	37
BLOODY MARY WINGS	39
BUFFALO WINGS	41
DELICIOUS HONEY DIJON WINGS	42
SPICY PEACH CHICKEN WINGS	43
CILANTRO LIME CHICKEN WINGS	44
MONGOLIAN CHICKEN WINGS	46
ROOT BEER BBQ WINGS	48
BALSAMIC GLAZED WINGS	50
KOREAN BBQ WINGS	52
JACK DANIELS BBQ WINGS	53

BEFORE YOU GO FURTHER! — 55

WE NEED YOUR HELP... ☺	55

BEEF — 56

BEEF STIR FRY	57
BEEF TACO EGGROLLS	59
MONGOLIAN BEEF WITH GREEN BEANS	61
BEEF FRIED RICE	63
BEEF MEATBALLS	64
CARNE ASADA TACOS	65
CHICKEN FRIED STEAK	67
BEEF STUFFED ROASTED BELL PEPPERS	69
MINI MEATLOAF	70
BBQ BOURBON BACON BURGER	72

PORK — 74

BREADED PORK CHOPS	75
PARMESAN CRUSTED PORK CHOPS	76
GARLIC BUTTER PORK CHOPS	77
BACON WRAPPED PORK TENDERLOIN WITH APPLES AND GRAVY	78
EASY PORK TAQUITOS	80
BACON WRAPPED CAJUN JALAPEÑOS	81
BACON WRAPPED SHRIMP JALAPEÑOS	82

SEAFOOD — 83

SPICY CRUNCHY SHRIMP	84
CAJUN SHRIMP	85
CRISPY COCONUT SHRIMP WITH SPICY CITRUS SAUCE	86
SWEET CITRUS SALMON	88

GoWise USA Air Fryer Cookbook

SOY LEMON SUGAR SALMON	89
CRAB CAKE SLIDERS	90
CRAB FRIED RICE	91
LOBSTER TAILS WITH LEMON GARLIC BUTTER	92
KETO FRIENDLY SHRIMP SCAMPI	93
BACON WRAPPED SCALLOPS	94

SIDES — 95

ASPARAGUS WITH BASIL & OLIVE OIL	96
ASPARAGUS WITH LEMON PEPPER	97
ASPARAGUS WITH CARROTS	98
HONEY CARROTS	99
ASIAN STYLE CAULIFLOWER AND CARROTS	100
NON-FRIED PICKLES	101
GARLIC NON-FRIED PICKLES	102
SPICY NON-FRIED PICKLES	103
GOLDEN CRISP FRENCH FRIES	104
GOLDEN SCALLION GARLIC FRIES	105
PARMESAN FRIES	106
GARLIC PARMESAN FRIES	107
GARLIC PARMESAN JALAPEÑO FRIES	108
SWEET POTATO FRIES	109
SPICY SWEET POTATO FRIES	110
TRUFFLE PARMESAN FRIES	111
GARLIC PARMESAN ROASTED POTATOES	112
TURMERIC TOFU AND CAULIFLOWER RICE	113
FRIED RAVIOLI WITH MARINARA SAUCE	115
AVOCADO FRIES WITH LIME DIP	116
STUFFED MUSHROOMS	117
HONEY GLAZED BUTTON MUSHROOMS	118
ZUCCHINI FRIES	119
SHISHIDO PEPPERS WITH ASIAGO CHEESE	121
SALT & VINEGAR CHIPS	122
BEET CHIPS	123
POTATO CHIPS	124
PARMESAN POTATO CHIPS	125
GARLIC PARMESAN POTATO CHIPS	126
FRIED GREEN TOMATOES WITH SRIRACHA MAYONNAISE DIPPING SAUCE	127

DESSERT — 129

APPLE FRIES WITH WHIP CREAM CARAMEL SAUCE	130

PEANUT BUTTER AND BANANA BITES	131
NUTELLA AND BANANA SANDWICHES	132
DOUBLE CHOCOLATE BROWNIES	133
POPCORN	135
CARAMEL POPCORN	136
APPLE DUMPLINGS	137
FRUIT CRUMBLE MUG CAKE	138
CHOCOLATE CAKE	139
BAKED APPLE	140
SHORTBREAD COOKIES	141
FRIED BANANA S'MORE	142
MINI APPLE PIES	143
CHOCOLATE M&M COOKIES	144
BANANA CHURRO	145

WHAT'S NEXT ON THE LIST! 146

REVIEW TIME...	146
YOURS FOR LOOKING	147
METRIC VOLUME CONVERSIONS CHART	148
METRIC WEIGHT CONVERSION CHART	149
TEMPERATURE CONVERSION CHART	149

ABOUT THE AUTHOR 150

AIR FRYER CREATION RECIPES & NOTES:	151

GoWise or Go Home!!!

What We've Found That the GoWise Air Fryer Gives You

We found that your air fryer can give you a lot of value for the money. It features a nonstick pan under the basket to help make clean up a breeze. The nonstick pan catches oil that drips out of your food during the air frying process. This seems to also be a great feature that food falls down into and the great part is that it's very east to clean up.

The state of the art technology within your air fryer allows it to heat up rapidly. You can heat up your air fryer to its highest temperature in only a few minutes. That saves you time compared to a traditional oven, which can take a while to preheat.

From what we found by using it is that this air fryer seems to have your safety in mind as well. It includes an automatic standby mode that beeps when your food is cooked. It then shuts off the heat to keep your food from overcooking and burning. The cooking basket has a release button that make sure it isn't accidentally detached from the pan. This comes in handy especially if you have small children. You don't have to worry about your children pulling on the basket and spilling all the hot food in the pan below on themselves or you. The basket will stay attached to the pan until the release button is pressed so the hot oil stays contained.

Features

The Various Parts of Your Air Fryer

We've found that the GoWise air fryer is built with multiple features to make cooking not only convenient, but a breeze.

Control Panel: The control panel has presets that cook foods like chicken, shrimp, and beef at specific temperatures for the predetermined time to give you perfect results. You can also set the timer temperature manually with plus or mind buttons next to clearly marked time and temperature icons.

LCD: The LCD screen lets you know what presets you're using if you decide to go that route. It also tells you the temperature and cooking time.

Fryer Basket: The air fryer comes with a detachable fryer basket, so that you can easily pour out your food without excess oil dripping on it. It comes equipped with a release button to keep the oil from spilling out of the pan.

Pan: The nonstick pan can be detached from the fryer basket, and catches all the oil that drips through the holes in the basket

Presets: Your air fryer comes equipped with presets to make cooking easy. You have presets for fries, chicken, steak, shrimp, pork, cake, fish, and warm. The warm preset warms food for a few minutes making it great for reheating things.

How to Use

The Steps to Making Food in Your Air Fryer

1. Always have your air fryer on an even and flat surface when using it. The fryer needs to be on a heat resistant surface, because it gets hot and can melt things.
2. Attach the basket to the pan.
3. Put whatever ingredients you're using into the basket and then place the attached basket and pan in the air fryer... push the start button.
4. Choose either one of the presets or set the temperature and cooking time manually using the plus and minus buttons.
5. When everything is set, push start again, to start the cooking process.
6. When the cooking process starts you'll see both the heat and fan icons blink. This means the temperature is rising and hot air is moving around and circulating.
7. Some recipes ask you to flip the food or shake the basket during the cooking process. You need to pull out the pan using the handle and gently shake it. Make sure you don't press the basket release button while shaking the basket and pan.
8. When the machine is done cooking your food it will make five beeps. The fan icon will then turn off.
9. Gently remove the pan with basket attached and put the pan down on a pot holder.
10. Hold the release button down on the fryer basket and pull the handle to remove the basket.
11. Place the cooked food on a plate or in a bowl to serve.

Cleaning is a Breeze

How to Make Sure Your Air Fryer Stays Clean

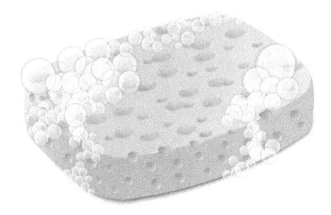

We've found that cleaning your GoWise Air Fryer Is not only incredibly simple, but easier than we expected. Make sure you wait until your air fryer has cooled off before cleaning it. Use a moist towel to clean off the outside parts of the fryer. Use either a slightly wet non-abrasive cloth or sponge to clean the inside of the fryer.

If you want to clean the heating coil use a cleaning brush to gently get rid of any debris. Use hot water, a non-abrasive sponge, and some soap to get the basket and pan clean. If you have food debris stuck on either use a little degreasing dish soap. If there's anything that is really stuck on particles in the pan, soak it in hot water for a while. You can also place the basket in your dishwasher, but you must remove the handle using a wrench to get the bolts loose so you can remove the screws. **The handle isn't dishwasher safe.**

Cooking Tips

How to Optimize the Use of Your Air Fryer

1. If you like your food really crispy...Get a kitchen spray bottle. It's easier to spray your food with oil than coating it with any other method. Spray bottles disperse oil better so you don't need to use as much to coat your food.

2. Put a little oil in the pan when you cook foods with high fat. This is something you should use for food like sausage and bacon because it helps to stop the grease that drips down from smoking.

3. Ideally let food come up to room temperature before placing it in your air fryer. Room temperature food cooks faster and ends up crispier than foods that are colder.

4. Use parchment paper or aluminum for oil for easier basket cleanup your parchment paper or aluminum foil for easier basket cleanup. Make sure that the aluminum foil or parchment paper doesn't cover the entire bottom of the basket because this will restrict airflow and stop your food cooking properly.

5. Shake the basket. Shaking your basket during the cooking process allows the food to cook more evenly.

6. Don't overfill your basket. Overfilling your basket won't get enough heat flowing to the food to cook evenly. Food will take longer to cook, and won't end up as crispy.

7. Try using the settings that are pre-set for different foods such as: fries, chicken, steak, shrimp, fish, pork, cake, pork and cake. There is even a warm setting to keep your food warm.

Let the Cooking Begin!

We've prepared this book for you so that you can enjoy everything about the air fryer you have in your kitchen. We made it really easy to navigate through this booklet and to help you out, we added measuring conversion chart at the end of this publication so you can take the guessing out of the equation. Also look in the back for out Bonus Marinade section for you to get creative with the meats and vegetables that you will be preparing for yourself, family and friends! Now turn the page and enjoy!

Sarah Conner

Chicken

Chicken Parma

This is an easy version of the Italian classic. The chicken comes out crunchy and delicious. The marinara sauce adds the perfect tangy flavor that's only made better by the creamy mozzarella.

Prep Time: 15 Minutes / Cook Time: 18 Minutes / Servings: 4

Ingredients:
2, 8 oz. organic chicken breast, sliced in half
6 tbsps. seasoned panko breadcrumbs
2 tbsps. grated fat-free Parmesan cheese
1 tbsp. olive oil
6 tbsps. Fat-free mozzarella cheese
1/2 cup marinara
cooking spray with olive oil

Directions:
- Spray the basket of your air fryer with cooking spray and preheat to 390F for at least 9 minutes.
- While the air fryer is preheating, mix together the bread crumbs and parmesan. Place the melted butter or olive oil in a separate bowl.
- Brush the chicken with a light coat of the olive oil. Then dredge the chicken in the parmesan breadcrumb mixture.
- Place 2 pieces of chicken in the basket of the preheated air fryer. Spray a little cooking spray on top of the basket.
- Cook the 2 chicken pieces for 6 minutes and then flip them. Top the chicken with 1 tbsp. sauce and 1 ½ tbsp. cheese. Cook for about 3 more minutes, until the cheese melts.
- Keep the cooked chicken warm while you repeat the same steps with the remaining 2 pieces of chicken.

Honey Sriracha Hot Wings

These wings have a great sweet and spicy flavor. The honey gives you a nice sweetness that helps to reduce the bold spicy flavor of the Sriracha. Best of all, they cook quickly, and you save time by making the sauce while the wings are cooking.

Prep Time: 15 Minutes / Cook Time: 18 Minutes / Servings: 2

Ingredients:
1 lb. organic chicken wings, tips removed, and wings cut into individual drumettes and flats.
1/4 cup honey
2 tbsps. Sriracha sauce
1 1/2 tbsps. light soy sauce
1 tbsp. organic butter
juice of 1/2 a lime
cilantro, chives, or scallions for garnish

Directions:
> Preheat your air fryer to 360F.
> Once the air fryer is preheated, cook the chicken wings in the basket for 30 minutes. Flip the wings every 7 minutes to ensure they cook evenly.
> While the wings are cooking, mix the honey, Sriracha, soy, butter, and lime juice in a sauce pan and bring them to a boil. Allow them to boil for 3 minutes and then take them off the heat.
> Toss the cooked wings in the sauce. Top with garnish and serve immediately.

Tandoori Chicken

This recipe is filled with all the delicious tandoori flavor you'd find at an Indian restaurant. The secret is the 2 different marinades. They build a full flavor within the chicken that you're going to love...

Prep Time: 12 Hours 20 Minutes / Cook Time: 20 Minutes / Servings: 4

Ingredients:
4 organic chicken legs with thigh

Marinade 1:
3 tsps. Ginger paste
3 tsps. Garlic paste
Salt to taste
3 tbsps. Lemon juice

Marinade 2:
2 tbsps. Tandoori masala powder
1 tsp. Roasted cumin powder
1 tsp. Garam masala powder
2 tsps. Red chili powder
1 tsp. Turmeric powder
4 tbsps. Hung curd -
2 tsps. Kasuri Methi
1 tsp. Black pepper powder
2 tsps. Coriander powder

Directions:
> Use a sharp knife to cut slits in the chicken.
> Mix all the ingredients together for marinade one in a bowl and add in the chicken.
> Cover the bowl and allow it to marinate for 15 minutes
> Mix together the ingredients for marinade 2 and pour it into the bowl with the chicken.
> Mix everything together until well combined.

- Cover the bowl and allow it to marinate in the refrigerator for 12-24 hours
- Use aluminum foil to line the basket of your air fryer.
- Preheat your air fryer to 290F.
- Add in the chicken and let it cook for 18-20 minutes. The chicken should be browned and lightly charred.

Parmesan Garlic Chicken Wings

This is a delicious Italian version of chicken wings. The parmesan gives the wings a salty cheesy flavor, and a crispy crunch, while the garlic adds an aromatic flavor that compliments the cheese.

Prep Time: 5 Minutes / Cook Time: 24 Minutes / Servings: 4

Ingredients:
2 lbs. organic wings + drumettes
3/4 cup grated fat-free parmesan cheese
2 tsps. minced garlic
2 tsps. fresh parsley, chopped
1 tsp. salt
1 tsp. pepper
Cooking spray with olive oil

Directions:
- Spray the basket of your air fryer with cooking spray.
- Preheat your air fryer at 400F for 4 minutes.
- Use a paper towel to pat the chicken wings dry.
- Combine the parmesan, garlic, salt, pepper, and parsley in a bowl. Make sure they're well mixed.
- Place the chicken wings in the bowl with the seasoning and toss until the chicken wings are well coated.
- Put the chicken wings in the air fryer and allow them to cook for 12 minutes before flipping them and allowing them to cook for about another 12 minutes. Check on the wings during the last few minutes to make sure they don't burn.
- Top the cooked wings with a little more parmesan and a few pieces of parsley as a garnish. Serve immediately.

Parmesan Garlic Chicken Tenders

These chicken wings have a cheesy crispy coating. The panko breadcrumbs make the tenders so light and crispy, while the parmesan adds the perfect amount of salty cheesiness, and the garlic's aromatic flavor balances the flavor of the cheese. Serve with your favorite dipping sauce. We recommend marinara.

Prep Time: 5 Minutes / Cook Time: 12 Minutes / Servings: 4

Ingredients:
8 raw organic chicken tenders
1 organic egg
2 tbsps. of water
Cooking spray with olive oil
Dipping sauce of your choice

The Parmesan Garlic Coating:
1 cup panko breadcrumbs
1/2 tsp. salt
1/4 tsp. ground black pepper, or more to taste
1 tsp. garlic powder
1/2 tsp. onion powder
1/4 cup organic parmesan cheese

Directions:
- Spray the basket of your air fryer with cooking spray.
- Preheat your air fryer to 400F.
- Mix together the parmesan garlic coating ingredients in a large bowl.
- Whisk together the water and egg in a medium bowl.
- Dip the chicken in the egg bowl and then in the parmesan bowl. Make sure the chicken is well coated.
- Place the chicken in your air fryer and cook for 12 minutes, flipping halfway through.
- Serve with your favorite dipping sauce.

Pizza Stuffed Chicken Thighs

This is a healthy and delicious way to get your pizza fix. Instead of carb heavy pizza crust, everything goes right into a chicken thigh. Turkey pepperoni, cheese, and pizza sauce give you that pizza flavor you crave without the guilt.

Prep Time: 10 Minutes / Cook Time: 15 Minutes / Servings: 3

Ingredients:
5 boneless, skinless, organic chicken thighs
½ cup pizza sauce
15 slices turkey pepperoni
½ small red onion, sliced
5 oz. sliced fat-free mozzarella cheese
½ cup fat-free shredded cheese for topping

Directions:
- Preheat your air fryer at 370F.
- Spray the basket of your air fryer with cooking spray.
- Put the chicken thighs in the middle of 2 pieces of parchment paper. Pound the chicken until it thins out.
- Spread the pizza sauce on one side of the chicken then top it with 3 pieces of pepperoni and a couple pieces of onion.
- Place a slice of cheese on top of the pizza sauce, onion, and pepperoni.
- Fold the chicken over and use a toothpick to secure it shut.
- Cook the chicken thighs for 6 minutes and then flip for another 6 minutes. Place another piece of cheese on top of the thighs and cook for an additional 3 minutes.
- Remove the toothpicks and serve immediately.

Thai Chicken Eggrolls

These eggrolls make a tasty and healthy dinner or appetizer. They're filled with chicken, bell pepper, carrots, and green onions, as well as peanut sauce for flavor. They're easy to make and cook quickly

Prep Time: 10 Minutes / Cook Time: 8 Minutes / Servings: 4

Ingredients:
4 egg roll wrappers
2 cups organic rotisserie chicken, shredded
¼ cup Thai peanut sauce
1 medium carrot, very thinly sliced
3 green onions, chopped
¼ red bell pepper, julienned
non-stick cooking spray with olive oil or sesame oil

Thai Peanut Sauce:
¾ cup light coconut milk
½ cup creamy peanut butter
2 tbsps. sesame oil
¼ cup fresh lime juice
2 tbsps. low-sodium soy sauce
3-4 Thai chili peppers, seeded, deveined & chopped or 1½ tsps. crushed red pepper flakes
1 tbsp. rice wine vinegar
1 tbsp. honey
¼ tsp. ground ginger

Directions:
› Preheat your air fryer to 390F.
› Place the egg roll wrappers flat on a dry, clean surface.
› Put ¼ of all the vegetables on the bottom 3rd of one egg roll wrappers. Top the vegetables with a quarter of the chicken.
› Use water to make the edges of the wrapper lightly moist. Use the moistened edges to fold the sides of the egg roll towards the middle. Roll it

up tightly. Complete the same process with the other wrappers. Make sure you keep the finished egg rolls under a damp paper towel.
- Coat the egg rolls with cooking spray on all sides.
- Cook the egg rolls for about 6-8 minutes. The egg rolls will turn a nice golden brown and become crispy when done.
- Serve with a side of the peanut sauce.

Chicken Nuggets

Kids love chicken nuggets, but you don't always know what goes into them. Now, you can make delicious chicken nuggets at home with a few ingredients. Take pride in knowing what's going into the food you feed your family.

Prep Time: 12 Minutes / Cook Time: 8 Minutes / Servings: 4

Ingredients:
16 oz. organic skinless boneless chicken breasts, cut into 1-inch pieces
½ tsp. kosher salt and black pepper, or more to taste
2 tsps. olive oil
6 tbsps. whole wheat Italian seasoned breadcrumbs
2 tbsps. panko breadcrumbs
2 tbsps. grated fat-free parmesan cheese
Cooking spray with olive oil
your favorite dipping sauce

Directions:
- Preheat your air fryer to 400F.
- Salt and pepper both sides of the chicken.
- Mix the cheese, panko, and breadcrumbs in a bowl. Spray olive oil in another bowl.
- Put the chicken in the bowl with olive oil and cut the chicken with the olive oil.
- Then place the chicken in the other bowl and coat it with the mixture.
- Put the nuggets in your air fryer and spray the top with a little olive oil spray. Cook the nuggets for 8 minutes, making sure to flip them after 4 minutes. The nuggets will be golden brown when ready.
- Serve with dipping sauce of your choice.

Roast Chicken

This is one of the easiest ways to make delicious roast chicken. The seasoning gives it a delicious aromatic flavor that you'll love. There's very little work on your part. So, sit back, relax, and get ready to enjoy some delicious, juicy chicken

Prep Time: 10 Minutes / Cook Time: 1 Hour / Servings: 4-6

Ingredients:
1 organic whole chicken, 4 to 5 pounds
2 tsps. Light Mrs. Dash
2 tsps. sea salt
1 tsp. garlic powder
1 tsp. smoked paprika
1 tsp. dry mustard
½ tsp. black pepper

Directions:
- Preheat your air fryer to 350F.
- Rinse the chicken and pat it dry.
- Mix all the ingredients except for the chicken in a bowl.
- Rub the spice mixture all over the chicken.
- Put the chicken in your air fryer, breast side down, and cook it for 30 minutes.
- Flip the chicken over and cook it for an additional 30 minutes.
- Allow the chicken to rest for 10 minutes before you cut into it.

Classic Fried Chicken Thighs

Enjoy delicious fried chicken without the guilt. You get crispy fried chicken without any oil needed. The seasoning gives it a delicious southern flavor that you'll love. Enjoy a couple extra pieces of fried chicken without any guilt

Prep Time: 5 Minutes / Cook Time: 25 Minutes / Servings: 4

Ingredients:
1/2 cup whole-wheat flour
1 organic egg, beaten
4 small organic chicken thighs
1 1/2 tbsps. Old Bay Cajun Seasoning
1 tsp. seasoning salt

Directions:
- Preheat your air fryer to 390F.
- Place the flour, Cajun seasoning, and salt in a bowl and mix it together using a whisk.
- Coat the chicken with the seasoning mixture. Then dip it in the beaten egg and coat it with more of the seasoning mixture. Remove any extra flour.
- Put the chicken in your air fryer and cook it for 25 minutes.
- Serve immediately.

Nashville Hot Fried Chicken

Nashville hot fried chicken is the latest food craze. You get all the crispy deliciousness of fried chicken, but with the spicy kick. This is the fried chicken for spicy food lovers. Make sure you have a glass of milk handy when you eat this.

Prep Time: 5 Minutes / Cook Time: 25 Minutes / Servings: 4

Ingredients:
1, 4-pound organic chicken, cut into 6 pieces, 2 breasts, 2 thighs and 2 drumsticks
2 organic eggs
1 cup low-fat buttermilk
2 cups whole wheat flour
2 tbsp. paprika
1 tsp. garlic powder
1 tsp. onion powder
2 tsps. salt
1 tsp. freshly ground black pepper
Olive oil

Hot Sauce:
1 tbsp. cayenne pepper
1 tsp. salt
¼ cup Olive oil

4 slices wheat bread
dill pickle slices
cooking spray with olive oil

Directions:
- Spray the basket of your air fryer with cooking spray.
- Preheat your air fryer to 370F.
- Place the buttermilk and eggs in a bowl and whisk them together. Put the paprika, garlic and onion powder, salt, black pepper, and flour in a larger re-sealable plastic bag. Dip the chicken in the egg mixture and place it in the bag with seasoning. Seal the bag and shake it to coat the chicken. Repeat the process a second time.

- Spray a small amount of vegetable oil on the chicken.
- Cook the chicken in 2 separate batches for 20 minutes, making sure to flip the chicken after 10 minutes. When the 2nd batch is cooked reduce the air fryer temperature to 340F. Flip the chicken that's in the air fryer and add the remaining chicken on top. Cook all of the chicken for an additional 7 minutes.
- Towards the end of the cooking process, put the ¼ cup of oil in a small sauce pan and heat it on medium-high heat. Once the oil is hot, add in the remaining hot sauce ingredient and whisk everything together until it becomes a smooth sauce. Be careful because the seasoning will sizzle when it hits the hot oil.
- Put the white bread on a plate and place the chicken on top of it. Use a brush to spread the hot sauce over the chicken. Top the chicken with pickles and serve.

Honey Garlic Chicken Wings

These wings have a great mix of sweet and savory. The honey adds a delicious, rich, sweet flavor that's addictive. The garlic adds just enough savory flavor to balance out the sweetness of the honey. You'll want to make them again and again.

Prep Time: 10 Minutes / Cook Time: 35 Minutes / Servings: 2

Ingredients:
16 Pieces Organic Chicken Wings
3/4 cup Corn Starch
1/4 cup Clover Honey
1/4 cup Organic Butter
4 tbsps. Fresh Garlic, minced
1/2 tsp. Kosher Salt
1/8 cup Fresh Water or more as needed
Cooking spray with olive oil

Directions:
- Spray the basket of your air fryer with cooking spray.
- Preheat your air fryer to 380 F.
- Wash and pat the chicken wings dry. Put the wings in a bowl and pour in the corn starch. Toss the chicken with the corn starch until well coated.
- Put the chicken wings in your air fryer and cook for 25 minutes. Make sure you shake the basket in 5-minute intervals.
- Raise the temperature to 400F and cook for an additional 5-10 minutes, until the wings are brown and completely dry.
- While the wings are cooking, heat up a small sauce pan over low heat. Once warm, put in the butter and allow it to melt, then mix in the oil. Add in the garlic and allow it to cook for 5 minutes.
- Pour in the salt and honey and allow the mixture to simmer for 20 minutes, making sure you stir it occasionally. Pour in a little water to stop the mixture from hardening at the 15-minute mark.
- Put the cooked wings on a plate or in a bowl and pour the sauce on top.

Crispy Restaurant Style Chicken Sandwiches

Are you a fan of Chick Fil A's chicken sandwiches? This the recipe for you, because these tastes just like the ones you got there. Enjoy the delicious crispy restaurant taste from the comfort of your own home.

Prep Time: 10 Minutes / Cook Time: 16 Minutes / Servings: 4

Ingredients:
2 Boneless, Organic Skinless Chicken Breasts, pounded
1/2 cup Dill Pickle Juice
2 Organic Eggs
1/2 cup Skim Milk
1 cup Wheat Flour
2 tbsp. Powdered Sugar
1 tsp. Paprika
1 tsp. Sea Salt
1/2 tsp. Freshly Ground Black Pepper
1/2 tsp. Garlic Powder
1/4 tsp. Ground Celery Seed ground
1 tbsp. Extra Virgin Olive Oil extra virgin
1 Oil Mister
4 Wheat Hamburger Buns, toasted
8 Dill Pickle Chips
Cooking spray with olive oil

Directions:
- Put the chicken in a re-sealable plastic bag and pound the chicken until it's ½ inch thick. Cut the pounded breasts in half.
- Put the chicken in another re-sealable plastic bag and add in the pickle juice. Seal the bag and shake it to coat the chicken. Allow it to marinate in the refrigerator for a minimum of 30 minutes.
- Spray the basket of your air fryer with cooking spray
- Preheat your air fryer to 340 F.

- Beat together the eggs and milk in a medium sized bowl. Place all the spices and flour in another medium bowl and mix them together.
- Dip the chicken in the egg mixture and then coat it with the spice mixture. Shake off any excess flour.
- Spray the chicken with oil and then put it in your air fryer. Allow the chicken to cook for 6 minutes. After 6 minutes spray the chicken with more oil and flip it. Cook for an additional 6 minutes. Increase the temperature to 400F and continue to cook the chicken for 4 minutes, flipping halfway through.
- Place the cooked chicken on hamburger buns, top with 2 pickles chips and a little mayonnaise.
- Serve immediately.

BBQ Chicken

Now you can have healthy BBQ chicken with all the flavor. They air fryer leaves the chicken juicy and the skin crispy without the need for oil. The flavor of the BBQ sauce gets cooked into the meat for more intense flavor.

Prep Time: 15 Minutes / Cook Time: 25 Minutes / Servings: 4

Ingredients:
1, 3 ½ pound Organic chicken, cut into 8 serving pieces
1 tbsp. smoked paprika
2 tsps. kosher salt
1 tsp. garlic powder
1/2 tsp. freshly ground black pepper
1 tsp. light brown sugar
1 ½ cups BBQ Sauce of your choice, plus more for serving

Directions:
- Preheat your air fryer to 375F.
- Mix all the spices together in a bowl.
- Rub every piece of chicken with the mix of spices.
- Put the chicken, skin side down, in your air fryer and cook it for 20 minutes.
- Take the chicken out reduce the temperature to 350F and brush the chicken with BBQ sauce of your choice.
- Cook the chicken for 5-10 more minutes, until completely cooked.
- Serve the chicken with a side of your favorite BBQ sauce.

Spicy BBQ Chicken

This air fryer style spicy BBQ chicken leaves the chicken juicy and the skin crispy without the need for oil. The locked in flavor of the spicy BBQ sauce gets cooked deep into the meat for a more intensified flavor.

Prep Time: 15 Minutes / Cook Time: 25 Minutes / Servings: 4

Ingredients:
1, 3 ½ pound organic chicken, cut into 8 serving pieces
1 tbsp. smoked paprika
2 tsps. kosher salt
1 tsp. garlic powder
1/2 tsp. freshly ground black pepper
1/8 tsp. cayenne pepper
1 tsp. oregano
1 tsp. light brown sugar
1 ½ cups BBQ Sauce of your choice, plus more for serving

Directions:
- Preheat your air fryer to 375F.
- Mix all the spices together in a bowl.
- Rub every piece of chicken with the spice mixture
- Put the chicken, skin side down, in your air fryer and cook it for 20 minutes.
- Take the chicken out reduce the temperature to 350F and brush the chicken with the BBQ sauce of your choice.
- Cook the chicken for 5-10 more minutes, until completely cooked.
- Serve chicken with a side of your favorite BBQ sauce.

Crispy Chicken Breast

Enjoy all the crispy chicken you want without all the fat and oil. These crispy chicken breasts get a nice bit of flavor from the garlic.

Prep Time: 10 Minutes / Cook Time: 10 Minutes / Servings: 4

Ingredients:
1-pound organic boneless skinless chicken breasts
1 tbsp. olive oil

Breading:
¼ cup panko bread crumbs
½ tsp. salt
¼ tsp. black pepper
½ tsp. paprika
1/8 tsp. garlic powder
1/8 tsp. onion powder

Directions:
> Preheat your air fryer to 390F.
> Slice the chicken breasts in half. This will create 2 thin chicken breast that will cook quicker.
> Brush the breast with a coat of olive oil
> Mix all the breading ingredients together in a bowl. Dip the chicken breasts into the mixture until they're completely coated. Shake off any excess mixture from the chicken.
> Put the chicken in your air fryer and allow them to cook for 4 minutes, then flip them and cook for 2 additional minutes. Check to see if the chicken is done and cook for a few additional minutes if necessary.

Crispy Spicy Chicken Breast

Enjoy all the crispy chicken you want without all the fat and oil. These crispy chicken breasts get a nice bit of heat from the cayenne. Use less cayenne if you're not big on heat.

Prep Time: 10 Minutes / Cook Time: 10 Minutes / Servings: 4

Ingredients:
1-pound Organic boneless skinless chicken breasts
1 tbsp. olive oil

Breading:
¼ cup panko bread crumbs
½ tsp. salt
¼ tsp. black pepper
½ tsp. paprika
1/8 tsp. garlic powder
1/8 tsp. onion powder
¼ tsp. cayenne pepper

Directions:
- Preheat your air fryer to 390F.
- Slice the chicken breasts in half. This will create 2 thin chicken breast that will cook quicker.
- Brush the breast with a coat of olive oil
- Mix all the breading ingredients together in a bowl. Dip the chicken breasts into the mixture until they're completely coated. Shake off any excess mixture from the chicken.
- Put the chicken in your air fryer and allow them to cook for 4 minutes, then flip them and cook for 2 additional minutes. Check to see if the chicken is done and cook for a few additional minutes if necessary.

Jerk Chicken Wings

These chicken wings have all the spicy jerk flavor you can handle. The habanero makes them very spicy and the allspice, cinnamon, and brown sugar give them a deep, warm flavor. Be careful because your mouth might be on fire when you eat these! Wear gloves when handling the habanero because the oil can get on your skin and get in your eyes if you rub them after.

Prep Time: 2 hours 10 Minutes / Cook Time: 30 Minutes / Servings: 6

Ingredients:
3 pounds Organic chicken wings
2 tbsp. olive oil
2 tbsp. low-sodium soy sauce
6 cloves garlic, finely chopped
1 habanero pepper seeds and ribs removed finely chopped
1 tbsp. allspice
1 tsp. cinnamon
1 tsp. Cayenne pepper
1 tsp. white pepper
1 tsp. sea salt
2 tbsps. light brown sugar
1 tbsp. fresh thyme, finely chopped
1 tbsp. fresh ginger, grated
4 scallions, finely chopped
5 tbsps. Lime Juice
1/2 cup Red wine vinegar
Light Ranch or light blue cheese dressing

Directions:
> Combine all of the ingredients in a large bowl or large re-sealable plastic bag. Add in the chicken and shake if you're using a bag or toss the chicken if using a bowl.
> Cover the bowl and/or place the sealed bag in your refrigerator for 2-24 hours to marinate.
> Preheat your air fryer to 390F.
> Take the wings out of the liquid and use a paper towel to pat them dry

- Place the marinated chicken in your air fryer in 2 batches and cook for 14-16 minutes. Make sure you shake the basket halfway through.
- Serve immediately with a side of blue cheese or ranch dressing,

Bloody Mary Wings

Wings and alcohol are always a winning pair. The wings marinate in a delicious Bloody Mary sauce that includes vodka. The wings come out packed with all the boozy alcohol flavor you want.

Prep Time: 1 Hour 10 Minutes / Cook Time: 25 Minutes / Servings: 6

Ingredients:
3 lbs. organic chicken wings
celery salt, to taste
Freshly ground black pepper, to taste

Bloody Mary Sauce:
3 cups tomato juice
2/3 cup vodka
3/4 cup light brown sugar
1/3 cup Hot sauce, such as Tabasco
1 tbsp. horseradish
1 tbsp. Worcestershire sauce
Juice of 1 lemon
kosher salt, to taste
Freshly ground black pepper, to taste

Dip:
2/3 cup light sour cream
2 tsps. horseradish
2 tsps. chopped dill

Directions:
- Rinse the chicken wings and use a paper towel to pat them dry.
- Season the dry wings with celery salt and pepper
- Mix together the Bloody Mary ingredients in a large bowl. Reserve about 1 ½ cups for later.
- Add the wings to the bowl of Bloody Mary sauce. Toss the wings and submerge them in the sauce. Cover the bowl and place it in the refrigerator for at least 1 hour.

- Preheat your air fryer to 380F.
- Take the wings out of the bowl and pat the wings dry.
- Place the chicken wing in your air fryer and allow them to cook for 25 minutes, making sure to shake the basket at the halfway point.
- While the chicken wings are cooking, heat a medium sauce pan on medium heat and add the reserved Bloody Mary sauce. Let the sauce come to a simmer and then cover it. Let it continue cooking until it reduces by half.
- Place the dip ingredients in a bowl and use a whisk to combine them.
- Place the wings in a big bowl and pour the sauce over it. Toss the wings in the sauce until they're well coated.
- Serve immediately with a side of the dip.

Buffalo Wings

This is the classic Buffalo wings that you love. They're a beautiful mix of spicy and buttery. They make the perfect food for the next time you're watching sports. Add the brown sugar if you want a little sweetness.

Prep Time: 5 Minutes / Cook Time: 30 Minutes / Servings: 8

Ingredients:
4 pounds Organic Chicken Wing Sections
½ cup Frank's Red-Hot Cayenne Pepper Sauce
½ cup Organic Butter
1 tbsp. Worcestershire Sauce
2 tbsps. Light Brown Sugar, optional
1 tsp. Kosher Salt

Directions:
- Preheat your air fryer to 380F.
- Rinse the chicken wings and use a paper towel to pat them dry.
- Place the chicken wing in your air fryer and allow them to cook for 25 minutes, making sure to shake the basket at the halfway point.
- While the chicken wings are cooking, whisk together the remaining ingredients.
- After the 25 minutes shake the basket again and raise the temperature to 400F. Allow the chicken to cook for 5 additional minutes.
- Place the wings in a big bowl and pour the sauce over it. Toss the wings in the sauce until they're well coated.
- Serve immediately.

Delicious Honey Dijon Wings

Wings with honey Dijon glaze will give an exceptional flavor to your wings every time! This is a treat for anyone who is a lover of wings!

Prep Time: 5 Minutes / Cook Time: 30 Minutes / Servings: 8

Ingredients:
4 pounds Organic Chicken Wing Sections
½ cup Dijon Mustard
½ cup Organic Butter
1 tbsp. Honey
2 tbsps. Light Brown Sugar, optional
1 tsp. Kosher Salt

Directions:
- Preheat your air fryer to 380F.
- Rinse the chicken wings and use a paper towel to pat them dry.
- Place the chicken wings in your air fryer. Lightly spray with oil and allow them to cook for 25 minutes. Shake the basket at the halfway point.
- While the chicken wings are cooking, whisk together the remaining ingredients.
- After the 25 minutes, shake the basket again and raise the temperature to 400F. Allow the chicken to cook for 5 additional minutes.
- Place the wings in a big bowl and pour the sauce over it. Toss the wings in the sauce until they're well coated.
- Serve immediately.

Spicy Peach Chicken Wings

These wings have a great blend of fruity sweetness, as well as some sourness, and heat. The peach adds a lovely balance of sweet and sour to the wings. The hot sauce adds the heat you want that balances out the sweet and sour.

Prep Time: 10 Minutes / Cook Time: 30 Minutes / Servings: 6

Ingredients:
Kosher salt, to taste
1 tsp. smoked paprika
1/2 tsp. garlic powder
3 lbs. organic chicken wings, cut at joint
2 oz. organic butter
2 cloves garlic, chopped
1/2 cup peach preserves
1/4 cup hot sauce, like Tabasco
1 tbsp. low-sodium soy sauce

Directions:
- Preheat your air fryer to 380F.
- Rinse the chicken wings and use a paper towel to pat them dry.
- Combine the garlic powder and paprika
- Coat the chicken wings with the seasoning mix.
- Place the chicken wings in your air fryer and allow them to cook for 25 minutes, making sure to shake the basket at the halfway point.
- While the chicken wings are cooking, heat a medium sauce pan on medium heat and melt the butter along with the garlic.
- Mix in the soy sauce, hot sauce, and peach preserve. Allow the mixture to cook for about 5 minutes, until it becomes thick and syrupy.
- After the 25 minutes shake the basket again and raise the temperature to 400F. Allow the chicken to cook for 5 additional minutes.
- Place the wings in a big bowl and pour the sauce over it. Toss the wings in the sauce until they're well coated.
- Serve immediately.

Cilantro Lime Chicken Wings

These wings have a beautiful citrusy, spicy flavor. The lime adds a lovely citrus flavor that gives the wings a zip of tanginess. The cilantro adds freshness, the honey adds sweetness, and the hot sauce gives just enough heat to balance everything.

Prep Time: 10 Minutes / Cook Time: 30 Minutes / Servings: 6

Ingredients:
¼ cup extra-virgin olive oil
Juice of 2 limes
1 tsp. garlic powder
1 tsp. ground cumin
1/2 tsp. smoked paprika
3 lbs. organic chicken wings
kosher salt, to taste
Freshly ground black pepper, to taste

GLAZE:
4 tbsps. organic butter
2 tbsps. honey
1 tbsp. Hot sauce
Juice of 1 lime
2 tbsps. chopped cilantro

Directions:
- Preheat your air fryer to 380F.
- Rinse the chicken wings and use a paper towel to pat them dry.
- Put the paprika, lime juice, cumin, and garlic powder in a big bowl and use a whisk to mix them together. Place the chicken wings in the bowl and toss them in the mixture. Cover the bowl and allow the wings to marinate in the refrigerator for at least an hour.
- Take the wings out of the marinade and use a paper towel to pat them dry.
- Place the chicken wing in your air fryer and allow them to cook for 25 minutes, making sure to shake the basket at the halfway point.

- While the chicken wings are cooking, heat a small sauce pan on medium heat and melt the butter in it. Use a whisk to mix in the lime juice, hot sauce, and honey. Take the sauce off the heat and stir in the cilantro
- After the 25 minutes shake the basket again and raise the temperature to 400F. Allow the chicken to cook for 5 additional minutes. Season the wings with salt and pepper.
- Place the wings in a big bowl and pour the sauce over it. Toss the wings in the sauce until they're well coated.
- Serve immediately.

Mongolian Chicken Wings

These wings are a lovely combo of sweet and spicy. They taste like the Mongolian beef you find at a Chinese restaurant, but now with chicken. They get a delicious caramelized flavor after they've been placed under your broiler for a couple of minutes. Be careful because these wings are addictive.

Prep Time: 10 Minutes / Cook Time: 33 Minutes / Servings: 3

Ingredients:
1 1/2 lbs. organic chicken wings
Salt and pepper, to taste

Sauce:
1/4 cup low-sodium soy sauce
1/4 cup honey
2 tbsps. rice wine vinegar
1 tbsp. Sriracha
3 cloves garlic, minced
1 tbsp. grated fresh ginger

Green onions, for garnish
Sesame seeds, for garnish

Directions:
- Preheat your air fryer to 380F.
- Rinse the chicken wings and use a paper towel to pat them dry.
- Season the wings with salt and pepper.
- Place the chicken wings in your air fryer and allow them to cook for 25 minutes, making sure to shake the basket at the halfway point.
- While the chicken wings are cooking, add the sauce ingredients to a medium sauce pan and bring the mixture to a simmer. Once the mixture is simmering, lower the heat a little. Allow the mixture to cook for 10 minutes.
- After the 25 minutes, shake the basket again and raise the temperature to 400F. Allow the chicken to cook for 5 additional minutes.
- Preheat your broiler.

- Place the wings in a big bowl and pour the sauce over them. Toss the wings in the sauce until they're well coated. Place the coated wings on a baking sheet and place them under the broiler for 2-3 minutes, until the wings caramelize.
- Serve immediately.

Root Beer BBQ Wings

These wings have a great sweet BBQ sauce. The root beer adds a great aromatic flavor to the BBQ sauce. The flavors intensify when the wings and sauce caramelize after they're placed under your broiled for a couple of minutes. One batch of these sweet wings might not be enough!

Prep Time: 10 Minutes / Cook Time: 33 Minutes / Servings: 6

Ingredients:
Sauce:
3/4 cup root beer
1 cup ketchup
1 tbsp. light brown sugar
2 tbsps. honey
1 tbsp. Worcestershire sauce
Juice of 1 lime
1/2 tsp. garlic powder
1/2 tsp. onion powder

3 lb. organic chicken wings
kosher salt, to taste
Freshly ground black pepper, to taste

Directions:
- Preheat your air fryer to 380F.
- Rinse the chicken wings and use a paper towel to pat them dry.
- Season the wings with salt and pepper to taste.
- Place the chicken wings in your air fryer and allow them to cook for 25 minutes, making sure to shake the basket at the halfway point.
- While the chicken wings are cooking, add the sauce ingredients to a medium sauce pan, whisk them together, and heat on medium-low heat. Bring the mixture to a simmer. Once the mixture is simmering, allow the mixture to cook until it reduces a little, around 8-10 minutes.
- After the 25 minutes shake the basket again and raise the temperature to 400F. Allow the chicken to cook for 5 additional minutes.
- Preheat your broiler.

- Place the wings in a big bowl and pour the sauce over it. Toss the wings in the sauce until they're well coated. Place the coated wings on a baking sheet and place them under the broiler for 2-3 minutes, until the wings caramelize.
- Serve immediately.

Balsamic Glazed Wings

These wings have a delicious sweet and tangy flavor. As the sauce reduces down, the sweetness of the honey, and the tanginess of the balsamic vinegar intensify. The garlic brings a little savory flavor to balance out the sweetness of the glaze. The flavor goes into hyper drive when the wings and glaze caramelize under your broiler.

Prep Time: 10 Minutes / Cook Time: 35 Minutes / Servings: 4

Ingredients:
Glaze:
Freshly ground black pepper, to taste
1 1/4 cups balsamic vinegar
2 tbsps. honey
3 cloves garlic, finely minced

2 lbs. organic party chicken wings
1 tbsp. Italian seasoning
Salt and pepper, to taste
Light Caesar dressing, for dipping

Directions:
- Preheat your air fryer to 380F.
- Rinse the chicken wings and use a paper towel to pat them dry.
- Season the wings with Italian seasoning, salt, and pepper.
- Place the chicken wings in your air fryer and allow them to cook for 25 minutes, making sure to shake the basket at the halfway point.
- While the chicken wings are cooking, add the sauce ingredients to a medium sauce pan, whisk them together, and heat on medium-low heat. Bring the mixture to a simmer. Once the mixture is simmering, allow the mixture to cook until it reduces a little, around 8-10 minutes.
- After the 25 minutes shake the basket again and raise the temperature to 400F. Allow the chicken to cook for 5 additional minutes.
- Preheat your broiler.
- Place the wings in a big bowl and pour the sauce over it. Toss the wings in the sauce until they're well coated. Place the coated wings on a baking

sheet and place them under the broiler for 5 minutes, until the wings caramelize.
- Serve immediately with a side of Caesar dressing if you'd like.

Korean BBQ Wings

These wings have a sweet and spicy BBQ sauce. The Sriracha gives the sauce some heat that's balanced by the sweetness of the honey. The lemon gives the sauce a little freshness to balance the sweet and spicy.

Prep Time: 10 Minutes / Cook Time: 35 Minutes / Servings: 3

Ingredients:
1 1/2 lbs. organic chicken wings and drumettes
kosher salt, to taste
Freshly ground pepper, to taste

BBQ Sauce:
1/4 cup ketchup
1/4 cup Sriracha
2 tbsps. honey
1 tsp. lemon juice

Toasted sesame seeds, for garnishing

Directions:
- Preheat your air fryer to 380F.
- Rinse the chicken wings and use a paper towel to pat them dry.
- Season the wings with salt, and pepper to taste.
- Place the chicken wings in your air fryer and allow them to cook for 25 minutes, making sure to shake the basket at the halfway point.
- While the chicken wings are cooking, add the sauce ingredients to a medium sized bowl, whisk them together, until the sauce becomes smooth.
- After the 25 minutes, shake the basket again and raise the temperature to 400F. Allow the chicken to cook for 5 additional minutes.
- Place the wings in the bowl with the sauce. Toss the wings in the sauce until they're well coated.
- Serve immediately with a garnish of sesame seeds.

Jack Daniels BBQ Wings

These wings have a delicious boozy BBQ sauce. The Jack Daniels gives the sauce a deep caramel flavor. You'll want a nice glass of whiskey to go with these finger-licking good wings.

Prep Time: 10 Minutes / Cook Time: 35 Minutes / Servings: 6

Ingredients:
3 lbs. organic chicken wings, (split at the joints, tips removed)
kosher salt, to taste
Freshly ground black pepper, to taste

BBQ Sauce:
2 tbsps. extra-virgin olive oil
1/2 yellow onion, minced
2 1/2 cups ketchup
1/4 cup molasses
1/3 cup apple cider vinegar
1/4 cup light brown sugar, packed
2 tbsps. tomato paste
1/4 cup Worcestershire sauce
1/3 cup Jack Daniel's whiskey

Directions:
- Preheat your air fryer to 380F.
- Rinse the chicken wings and use a paper towel to pat them dry.
- Season the wings with salt, and pepper to taste.
- Place the chicken wings in your air fryer and allow them to cook for 25 minutes, making sure to shake the basket at the halfway point.
- While the chicken wings are cooking, pour the olive oil in a medium sauce pan, and heat on medium heat. Put in the onions and cook until they become soft. Mix in the garlic and allow it to cook for 30 seconds, until it's fragrant. Then add in the remaining sauce ingredients and allow it to come to a simmer. Simmer the sauce for about 5-10 minutes, until it reduces a little and the flavors come together.

- After the 25 minutes shake the basket again and raise the temperature to 400F. Allow the chicken to cook for 5 additional minutes.
- Place the wings in a bowl and pour in the sauce. Toss the wings in the sauce until they're well coated.
- Serve immediately.

Sarah Conner

Before You Go Further!

We Need Your Help... ☺

PLEASE LEAVE US AN AMAZON REVIEW!

If you were pleased with our book then leave us a review on Amazon where you purchased this book! **Simply click the link**, scroll to the bottom & review!

>>>   Amazon.com/dp/B07F1S5ZZD   <<<

In the world of an author who writes books independently, your reviews are not only touching but important so that we know you like the material we have prepared for "you" our audience! So, leave us a review...we would love to see that you enjoyed our book!

If for any reason that you were less than happy with your experience then send me an email at **Info@RecipeNerds.com** and let me know how we can better your experience. We always come out with a few volumes of our books and will possibly be able to address some of your concerns. Do keep in mind that we strive to do our best to give you the highest quality of what "we the independent authors" pour our heart and tears into.

Hello all...I am very excited that you have purchased one of my publications. Please feel free to give us an amazon review where you purchased the book! If you already have, then I thank you for your many great reviews and comments! With a warm heart! ~Alicia Patterson "Personal & Professional Chef"

Beef

Beef Stir Fry

You get to make delicious beef stir fry without the need for a wok. This dish is really easy to make and creates a healthy dish your whole family will love. The homemade sauce really brings the dish together and gives the dish a delicious savory flavor.

Prep Time: 30 Minutes / Cook Time: 13 Minutes / Servings: 4

Ingredients:
1 lb. of organic beef sirloin, cut into 2-inch strips
1½ lb. of broccoli florets
1 red pepper, cut into strips
1 green pepper, cut into strips
1 yellow pepper, cut into strips
½ cup of onion, cut into strips
½ cup of red onion, cut into strips
1 tbsp. stir fry oil
2 cups cooked brown rice

Sauce:
¼ cup of hoisin sauce
2 tsps. of minced garlic
1 tsp. of sesame oil
1 tbsp. of soy sauce
1 tsp. of ground ginger
¼ cup of water

Directions:
> Mix all the sauce ingredients together in a bowl. Add beef and toss it until it's well coated. Cover the bowl and refrigerate for 20 minutes.
> While the beef is marinating, preheat your air fryer to 200F.
> Toss the vegetables with the stir fry oil.
> Place the vegetables in your preheated air fryer and allow them to cook for 5 minutes, until soft. If the vegetables are still somewhat firm, cook them for 2 additional minutes.
> Set the cooked vegetables aside in a bowl.

- Raise the temperature on your air fryer to 360F. Add in the meat when it's done marinating. Allow the beef to cook for 4 minutes. If the beef isn't cooked to your liking, flip it over and cook for 2 more minutes.
- Place the rice in 4 bowls and top it with the beef and vegetables.

Beef Taco Eggrolls

Taco Tuesday move on over! These eggrolls have all the ground beef taco taste you want incased in an eggroll. They're easy to make and will make you rethink your love for regular tacos.

Prep Time: 15 Minutes / Cook Time: 25 Minutes / Servings: 4

Ingredients:
1 lb. 90% lean organic ground beef
16 egg roll wrappers
1/2 onion, chopped
1 can Cilantro Lime Rotel
1/2 can fat-free refried black beans
1/2 packet Taco Seasoning
1 cup reduced-fat shredded Mexican Cheese
1/2 cup whole kernel corn
1 tbsp. olive oil
2 garlic cloves, chopped
salt and pepper to taste

1 tsp. chopped cilantro, optional
Cooking spray with olive oil

Directions:
- Preheat your air fryer to 400F.
- Use cooking spray to coat a skillet and heat the skillet on medium-high heat. Put In the onions and garlic, and allow them to cook until they become fragrant, a couple of minutes at most.
- Put in the beef, taco seasoning, salt and pepper, and allow the mixture to cook until the beef has browned. Make sure you break the meat up into small pieces while you cook it.
- Add in the corn, cilantro lime Rotel, and beans. Stir the mixture until it's well combined and then take it off the heat.
- You want to double wrap the eggrolls. Place the mixture in the middle of 8 doubled eggroll wrappers and top the mixture with cheese. Use water to make the edges of the wrapper lightly moist. Fold the sides of the

moistened edges of the egg roll towards the middle. Roll it up tightly. Complete the same process with the other wrappers.
- Brush the eggrolls with a light coating of olive oil and place them in your air fryer. Allow the eggrolls to cook for 8 minutes and then flip them over. Cook the eggrolls for 4 more minutes.
- Top the cooked eggrolls with cilantro and serve.

Sarah Conner

Mongolian Beef with Green Beans

This is just like the Mongolian beef you find at Chinese restaurants! The best part is you know exactly what goes into it and there's no unhealthy oil. It's got the crunchy texture you crave and packed with all the sweet and savory flavor you love.

Prep Time: 20 Minutes / Cook Time: 20 Minutes / Servings: 4

Ingredients:
Meat:
1 lb. Organic Flank Steak, thinly sliced in long chunks
1/4 Cup Corn Starch

Sauce:
2 tsps. Olive Oil
1/2 tsp. Ginger
1 tbsp. Minced Garlic
1/2 Cup low-sodium Soy Sauce
1/2 Cup Water
3/4 Cup Brown Sugar, Packed

2 cups Brown Rice, cooked
1 cup Green Beans, cooked
Green Onions, chopped

Directions:
- Preheat your air fryer to 390F.
- Place the beef in your air fryer and cook it for 10 minutes, flip it and cook for an additional 10 minutes.
- While the beef is cooking, heat a medium sauce pan on medium-high heat. Add in all the sauce ingredients and whisk them until the mixture comes to a low boil. Take the sauce off the heat.
- Put the cooked beef in a bowl and pour in the sauce. Allow the mixture to rest for about 10 minutes.
- While the beef is marinating, place the cooked rice in 4 bowls and top with the green beans.

- Remove the beef from the sauce and place it on top of rice. Sprinkle a little green onion on top. Drizzle on a little sauce if you'd like.
- Serve immediately.

Beef Fried Rice

You get to enjoy restaurant quality beef fried rice with this recipe. The best part is it costs a lot less and uses almost no oil. This makes the dish a lot healthier for you, which is always a nice bonus. The air fryer does all the hard work for this recipe. So find something good to watch while you wait for your delicious fried rice to cook!

Prep Time: 10 Minutes / Cook Time: 20 Minutes / Servings: 6

Ingredients:
3 cups cold brown rice, cooked
1 cup frozen peas and carrots
6 tbsps. Light soy sauce
1 tbsp. Olive oil
1/2 cup onion diced
1 cup organic beef
Cooking spray with olive oil

Directions:
- Preheat your air fryer to 360F.
- Put the rice in a bowl and mix in the oil and soy sauce. Make sure all ingredients are well mixed.
- Mix in the onions, beef, peas and carrots. Make sure all ingredients are well mixed again.
- Put the mixture in a non-stick pan that's small enough to fit in your air fryer, if you have one. Or spray cooking spray in a pan, small enough to fit in your air fryer, before adding in the mixture.
- Put the pan inside your air fryer and allow it cook for 20 minutes.
- Once it's cooked, place the rice in a bowl or on a plate to serve.

Beef Meatballs

This is a great way to make meatballs as an appetizer or for your family's spaghetti and meatballs dish. The meatballs come out perfectly cooked in no time at all and with no oil! That means your meatballs are much healthier. Grab some marinara sauce because these meatballs pair well with a little red sauce.

Prep Time: 10 Minutes / Cook Time: 20 Minutes / Servings: 2 dozen meatballs

Ingredients:
2 lbs. of lean organic ground beef
2 large organic eggs
1-1/4 cups Panko bread crumbs
1/4 cup chopped fresh parsley
1 tsp. dried oregano
1/4 cup grated fat-free parmigiano reggiano
1 small clove garlic chopped
salt and pepper to taste
Cooking spray with olive oil

Directions:
- Spray the basket of your air fryer with cooking spray.
- Preheat your air fryer to 350F.
- Mix together all the ingredients in a bowl, except for the cooking spray, until well mixed.
- Use your hands to make 2-inch round balls out of the mixture.
- Cook the meatballs in 2 batches for about 10-13 minutes. The meatballs should have a nice brown coloring. Flip them and cook for an additional 4-5 minutes. Repeat the same process with the 2nd batch.
- Place the cooked meatballs in some pasta sauce to absorb the flavor or serve them with your favorite pasta.

Carne Asada Tacos

There's nothing better than some juicy tacos on a nice warm day. The Carne Asada is marinated in citrus juice, brown sugar, chipotle, and spices to give it a depth of flavor. The Carne Asada comes juicy out of the air fryer! Add your favorite condiments and you've got the perfect tacos.

Prep Time: 3 Hours 15 Minutes / Cook Time: 20 Minutes / Servings:

Ingredients:
2 lbs. organic skirt steak, 1/2 thick or more
1 large Yellow Onion, thinly sliced
Your favorite taco condiments
salsa
Corn tortillas

Marinade:
4-5 whole Chipotle Peppers in Adobo, from a can
2 roasted Pasilla Peppers
1/2 cup Freshly Squeezed Orange Juice
1/4 cup Freshly Squeezed Lime Juice
1/4 cup Freshly Squeeze Lemon Juice
6 cloves Fresh Garlic
2 tbsps. Extra Virgin Olive Oil
1 cup Fresh Cilantro Leaves
2 tbsps. Light Brown Sugar
1 tbsp. Kosher Salt
2 tsps. Ground Cumin
2 tsps. Dried Oregano
1 tsp. Freshly Ground Black Pepper

Directions:
> Put all the marinade ingredients in a food processor or blender and blend until smooth. Save a ½ cup of the mixture to use for salsa.
> Place the onion and beef in a re-sealable plastic bag and pour in the marinade. Allow the mixture to marinate in the refrigerator for at least 3 hours.

- Preheat your air fryer to 400F.
- Put the steak and onions in your air fryer and allow it to cook for 7-10 minutes. Flip after about 4 minutes if you want your meat medium.
- Allow the steak to rest for 5 minutes before thinly slicing it.
- Place the sliced Carne Asada inside the tortillas, along with your favorite condiments.

Chicken Fried Steak

Fried chicken always hits the spot, and so does fried steak. This steak is breaded with panko for extra crispiness and topped with gravy, so you get a ton of flavor. You don't have to feel guilty about the gravy on your steak because the steak is cooked without all the oil.

Prep Time: 20 Minutes / Cook Time: 20 Minutes / Servings: 1

Ingredients:
6 oz. organic sirloin steak-pounded thin
3 organic eggs, beaten
1 cup whole-grain wheat flour
1 cup Panko break crumbs
1 tsp. onion powder
1 tsp. Garlic powder
1 tsp. salt
1 tsp. pepper

Gravy:
6 oz. organic ground sausage meat
2 tbsp. whole-grain wheat flour
2 cups Skim milk
1 tsp. pepper

Directions:
- Preheat your air fryer to 370F.
- Mix the panko, onion, garlic powder, salt, and pepper together in a bowl.
- Place the flour in a separate bowl, and the eggs in another bowl.
- Coat the steak with flour, then egg, and finally the panko.
- Place the steak in your air fryer and cook it for 12 minutes
- While the steak is cooking, heat a medium pan on medium heat. Add in the sausage and cook until the sausage is completely cooked. Keep 2 tbsps. of the fat in the pan and remove the rest.
- Mix in the flour and once the ingredients are well mixed slowly stir in the milk.

- Allow the mixture to cook until the milk thickens. Then season with the pepper. Cook for another 3 minutes to make sure the flour has fully incorporated.
- When the steak is cooked put it on a plate and top it with the gravy to serve.

Beef Stuffed Roasted Bell Peppers

This a classic dish that's easy to make. The beef is full of flavor - thanks to the seasoning and tomato sauce. The bell peppers intensify in flavor as they roast in the air fryer. The textures between the meat and the peppers are a perfect match.

Prep Time: 20 Minutes / Cook Time: 20 Minutes / Servings: 2

Ingredients:
2 medium green peppers, stems and seeds removed
½ medium onion, chopped
1 clove garlic, minced
1 tsp. olive oil
8 oz. lean organic ground beef
½ cup tomato sauce
1 tsp. Worcestershire sauce
½ tsp. salt
½ tsp. black pepper
4 ounces fat-free cheddar cheese, shredded

Directions:
> Put enough water in a medium size pot to cover the bell peppers. Salt the water and bring it to a boil. Once the water starts to boil, add in the bell peppers and cook for 3 minutes.
> Pat the cooked bell peppers dry with paper towels.
> Place the olive oil in a small pan and heat on medium heat. Add in the onions and garlic and cook until the onions are brown, about 5-7 minutes. Take the mixture off the heat and let it cool.
> Preheat your air fryer to 390F.
> In a large bowl, mix the Worcestershire sauce, garlic, onions, beef, half of the tomato sauce, salt, pepper, and half the cheese together.
> Stuff each pepper with half the mixture and top with the left-over tomato sauce and cheese.
> Place the peppers in your air fryer and cook for 15-20 minutes, until the beef is completely cooked.
> Serve immediately.

Mini Meatloaf

This is a personal sized version of the classic dish. The cornflakes give the meatloaf a nice crunch, which goes along with the sweet and savory flavor. The secret to this dish is re-glazing the top while the meatloaf is cooking.

Prep Time: 15 Minutes / Cook Time: 20 Minutes / Servings: 2

Ingredients:
Meatloaf:
1 lb. 90% lean organic ground beef
½ medium onion, chopped
1/3 cup Kellogg's corn flakes, crumbled
2 tsps. salt
2 tsps. freshly ground black pepper
1 tsp. minced garlic
6 oz tomato sauce
1 tsp. dried basil

Glaze:
5 tbsps. Heinz reduced-sugar ketchup
3 tsps. Splenda or Tuvia brown sugar blend
1 tbsp. Worcestershire sauce

2 mini loaf pans
½ tbsp. lightly dried or fresh chopped Parsley
Cooking spray with olive oil

Directions:
- Preheat your air fryer to 390F.
- Mix together all of the meatloaf ingredients in a bowl, until well combined.
- Spray the inside of the mini loaf pans with cooking spray.
- Split the meatloaf mixture between 2 mini loaf pans.
- Place the glaze ingredients in a bowl and mix them together.
- Brush a nice coating of the glaze on the sides and top of the loaves.
- Put the loaves in your air fryer for 20 minutes.
- Brush the loaves again with the glaze at the 10 and 16-minute marks.

- Top the cooked loaves with the parsley and allow them to rest for a couple minutes.
- Remove the loaves from the pans and serve immediately.

BBQ Bourbon Bacon Burger

This burger is a tangy delicious explosion in your mouth. The bacon cooks in brown sugar and bourbon to give it a sweet caramelized flavor. The burger itself has BBQ sauce in it for extra tanginess. The sauce is a lovely combo of mayo and BBQ sauce to give you that great BBQ taste you want.

Prep Time: 20 Minutes / Cook Time: 30 Minutes / Servings: 2

Ingredients:
Bacon:
1 tbsp. bourbon
2 tbsps. light brown sugar
3 strips organic maple bacon, cut in half

Burger Patties:
¾ lb. 80% lean organic ground beef
1 tbsp. minced onion
2 tbsps. BBQ sauce
½ tsp. salt
freshly ground black pepper

Sauce:
2 tbsps. BBQ sauce
2 tbsps. mayonnaise with olive oil
¼ tsp. ground paprika
freshly ground black pepper

2 slices fat-free Colby Jack or fat-free Monterey Jack cheese
2 whole wheat Kaiser rolls
lettuce and tomato for serving

Directions:
› Preheat your air fryer to 390F.
› Mix together the brown sugar and bourbon. Brush, it on one side of the bacon.

- Place the bacon in your air fryer with the brushed side up and cook for 4 minutes. Flip the bacon over and brush the other side with the brown sugar mixture. Allow it to cook for 4 more minutes.
- During the cooking process, Mix the burger ingredients in a bowl until well combined. Make the mixture into 2 patties using your hands.
- When the bacon is done reduce the temperature 370F and put the beef patties in. Cook the burgers for 15 minutes if you like them rare and up to 20 minutes if you like them well done. Make sure the burger is flipped about halfway through the cooking process
- While the patties are cooking, mix together the sauce ingredients in a bowl adding salt and pepper.
- When the burgers are cooked to how you want them, put a piece of cheese on top and allow them to cook for 1 more minute.
- Spread a nice layer of sauce on the inside of your buns and place the patties with melted cheese in the middle with your desired condiments.
- Serve immediately with the side of your choice.

Pork

Breaded Pork Chops

These breaded pork chops are full of taste without all the oil. The Dijon mustard gives the pork chops a tangy spicy flavor. The paprika adds a little smoky sweetness to balance the Dijon. The breadcrumbs give it a nice crunchy texture.

Prep Time: 10 Minutes / Cook Time: 16 Minutes / Servings: 4

Ingredients:
1/2 cup Dijon mustard
4 organic pork loin chops 3/4-inch thick
1 cup low-sodium Italian bread crumbs
1/2 tsp. salt
1/2 tsp. black pepper
1/4 tsp. cayenne pepper
1 tsp. smoked paprika
Cooking spray with olive oil

Directions:
> Spray the basket of your air fryer with cooking spray.
> Preheat your air fryer to 390F.
> Spread a layer of the mustard all over the pork chops
> Place the bread crumbs and spices in a bowl and mix them together.
> Coat the pork chops with the bread crumb mixture.
> Place the pork chops in your air fryer and cook them for 8 minutes per side.
> Serve immediately with the side of your choice.

Parmesan Crusted Pork Chops

These pork chops have a beautiful crust. The parmesan cheese adds a lovely salty flavor and the pork rinds add a lovely crunch. The chili powder adds the right amount of smokiness and savory flavor to the pork chop, as well.

Prep Time: 10 Minutes / Cook Time: 15 Minutes / Servings: 4

Ingredients:
4 thick center cut organic boneless pork chops
1/2 tsp. Salt
1/4 tsp. Pepper
1 tsp. Smoked Paprika
1/2 tsp. onion powder
1/4 tsp. chili powder
2 large organic eggs, beaten
1 cup low-fat pork rind crumbs
3 tbsps. grated fat-free parmesan cheese
Cooking spray with olive oil

Directions:
> Spray the basket of your air fryer with cooking spray.
> Preheat your air fryer to 400F.
> Place the pork rinds in a blender or food processer and pulse until they become crumbs.
> Mix together the paprika, onion powder, chili powder, pork rind crumbs, salt, pepper, and parmesan in a bowl.
> Put the beaten eggs in a different bowl.
> Coat the pork chops with the eggs, and then coat it with the pork rind mixture.
> Place the pork chops in your air fryer and cook for 12-15 minutes flipping halfway through.
> Serve immediately with a side of your choice.

Garlic Butter Pork Chops

These are great for anyone on the Whole30 Diet. The coconut oil adds a little exotic flavor to the dish, while the butter adds a rich creamy flavor. The garlic brings it all together with its aroma.

Prep Time: 1 Hour 10 Minutes / Cook Time: 16 Minutes / Servings: 4

Ingredients:
4 organic Pork Chops
1 tbsp. Organic Coconut Butter
1 tbsp. Coconut Oil
2 tsps. Garlic Cloves, grated
2 tsps. Parsley
Salt & Pepper, to taste

Directions:
› Mix together all the ingredients in a bowl except for the pork chops.
› Coat the pork chops with the mixture and wrap the pork chops in aluminum foil.
› Place the wrapped pork chops in the refrigerator for an hour.
› Take the pork chops out of the aluminum foil and sprinkle with any seasoning that may have stuck to the aluminum foil.
› Put the pork chops in your air fryer and cook them for 7 minutes. Flip the pork chops and cook them for an additional 8 minutes.
› Serve immediately with the side of your choice.

Bacon Wrapped Pork Tenderloin with Apples and Gravy

How do you make tender pork tenderloin better? You wrap it in bacon for an extra jolt of flavor. The apples and gravy add a nice mix of sweet and savory that compliments the salty, tangy flavor of the pork. Best of all, the whole dish takes less than an hour to make.

Prep Time: 15 Minutes / Cook Time: 30 Minutes / Servings: 4

Ingredients:
1 organic Pork Tenderloin
4 strips of organic bacon
2 tbsps. Dijon mustard

Apples with Gravy:
3 Granny Smith apples, cut in cubes
1 small onion or shallot, chopped
2 tbsps. organic butter, divided
1 tbsp. whole wheat flour
1 cup of vegetable broth
1 tsp. of Dijon mustard, optional
salt and pepper, to taste

Chopped rosemary or thyme, garnish
Cooking spray with olive oil

Directions:
- Spray the basket of your air fryer with cooking spray.
- Preheat your air fryer to 360F.
- Coat the pork tenderloin with the Dijon and then wrap the bacon around the tenderloin
- Place the tenderloin in your air fryer and cook for 15 minutes. Flip it over and cook for an additional 10-15 minutes, until fully cooked.

- While the tenderloin is cooking, heat a medium sauce pan on medium heat and then add in 1 tbsp. of butter. Melt the butter and add in the shallots. Allow the shallots to cook for 1-2 minutes, until they soften.
- Mix in the apples and allow the mixture to cook for 3-5 minutes, until the apples soften. Place the cooked mixture in a bowl and set it aside.
- Heat a small sauce pan on medium heat and add in the remaining butter and let it melt. Add in the flour and stir together until a paste begins to form
- Stir in the broth slowly allowing it to blend together with the flour. Mix in the mustard at this point if you're using it. Lower the heat to medium-low and cook, stirring occasionally, until the mixture starts to simmer, and bubbles start to pop up at the edges. Then pour in 1 cup of the apples. Let the mixture cook until it starts to thicken up.
- Allow the cooked pork to sit for 5 minutes before cutting it.
- Top the sliced pork with the apples and gravy.
- Garnish with thyme or rosemary and serve.

Easy Pork Taquitos

These taquitos are an easy to make meal or snack. They only have a few ingredients, but they're packed with flavor. Use leftover pork tenderloin or buy shredded pork from the store to make this really simple. The blend of cheese adds depth of flavor. Dip the taquitos in your salsa to finish...

Prep Time: 15 Minutes / Cook Time: 30 Minutes / Servings: 4

Ingredients:
30 oz. of cooked shredded organic pork tenderloin
2 1/2 cups shredded fat-free Mexican cheese blend
10 small wheat flour tortillas
Juice of 1 lime
Cooking spray with olive oil
Salsa for dipping, optional
Light Sour Cream, optional

Directions:
- Preheat your air fryer to 380F.
- Pour the lime juice over the pork and mix it together so all the pork is evenly coated with the juice.
- Microwave the tortillas in 2 even batches for 10 seconds under a damp paper towel.
- Add an even amount of cheese and pork to the middle of each tortilla.
- Be gentle as you roll the tortillas tightly.
- Line a pan with aluminum foil, spray it with cooking spray, and place the taquitos on it.
- Spray another coating of cooking spray on the taquitos.
- Place the taquitos in your air fryer and cook for 7-10 minutes, flipping halfway through.
- Serve the taquitos with a side of sour cream and salsa if you'd like.

Bacon Wrapped Cajun Jalapeños

Sometimes, Cajun is the way to go! Delicious and nutritious! Get on the band wagon and try these tasty tidbits. You'll be glad you did! Enjoy!

Prep Time: 8 Minutes / Cook Time: 15-18 Minutes / Servings: 4

Ingredients:
1 lb. organic bacon, raw uncooked
1 large sweet onion, cut into wedges
6 fresh jalapeno peppers
2 tsps. seafood seasoning, or
2 tsps. cayenne pepper

1 box of toothpicks, for wrapping

Directions:
- Preheat oven to 350 degrees F.
- Cut the bacon in half vertically then put on a plate.
- Cut and peel onion into wedges and separate, then put in a bowl.
- Wash the Jalapenos thoroughly, then slice into thirds long ways. Remove the seeds and place in a bowl.
- Start assembly with a slice of Jalapeno, and a slice of onion. Holding all in your hand, wrap bacon around and secure with a wooded toothpick. Repeat until all the ingredients have been used.
- Place on a baking sheet.
- Sprinkle with seasoning.
- Place in the oven and roast until bacon is slightly crisp. Roasting time may be adjusted.

Bacon Wrapped Shrimp Jalapeños

Delicious, succulent and melts in your mouth. Very tasty and flavorful treat that anyone will enjoy. Great for any appetizer and your friends will love you for it.

Prep Time: 8 Minutes / Cook Time: 15-18 Minutes / Servings: 4

Ingredients:
1 lb. large shrimp, peeled and cleaned
1 lb. organic bacon, raw uncooked
1 large sweet onion, cut into wedges
6 fresh jalapeno peppers
2 tsps. seafood seasoning, or
2 tsps. cayenne pepper

Directions:
- Preheat oven to 350 degrees F.
- Set shrimp aside in a bowl after peeled and washed. start an assembly line.
- Cut the bacon in half vertically then put on a plate.
- Cut and peel onion into wedges and separate, then put in a bowl.
- Wash the Jalapenos thoroughly, then slice into thirds long ways. Remove the seeds and place in a bowl.
- Start assembly with a piece of shrimp, a slice of Jalapeno, and a slice of onion. Holding all in your hand, wrap bacon around and secure with a wooded toothpick. Repeat with each shrimp.
- Place on a baking sheet.
- Sprinkle with seasoning.
- Place in the oven and roast until bacon is slightly crisp. Roasting time may be adjusted.

Sarah Conner

Seafood

Spicy Crunchy Shrimp

The shrimp stay nice and crunchy because the sauce is on the side for dipping. The panko provides the perfect crunch that make the shrimp taste like they're fried. The Sriracha in the sauce gives the heat you want to go with this delicious shrimp dish.

Prep Time: 10 Minutes / Cook Time: 8 Minutes / Servings: 4

Ingredients:
1 lb. organic raw shrimp, peeled and deveined
1 organic egg white
1/2 cup whole wheat flour
3/4 cup panko bread crumbs
1 tsp. paprika
Montreal Chicken Seasoning, to taste
salt and pepper, to taste
cooking spray with olive oil

Directions:
- Spray the basket of your air fryer with cooking spray.
- Preheat your air fryer to 400F.
- Put the flour, egg whites, and panko into 3 separate bowls. Add the rest of the seasoning to the bowl with panko and mix until well combined.
- Dip the shrimp in the flour, then egg whites, then the panko mixture.
- Place the shrimp in your air fryer and cook them for 4 minutes per side.
- While the shrimp are cooking, mix together the spicy sauce ingredients in a bowl.
- Serve the cooked shrimp with a side of the spicy sauce.

Cajun Shrimp

This is a really easy recipe to make. Once you toss the shrimp with the seasoning your work is done! You're rewarded with succulent shrimp that taste like you've made a trip to Louisiana. They go great with a side of rice.

Prep Time: 10 Minutes / Cook Time: 16 Minutes / Servings: 2

Ingredients:
1/2 lb. organic tiger shrimp, 16-20 count
1/4 tsp. cayenne pepper
1/2 tsp. old bay seasoning
1/4 tsp. smoked paprika
1 pinch of salt
1 tbsp. olive oil
Cooking spray with olive oil

Directions:
- Spray the basket of your air fryer with cooking spray.
- Preheat your air fryer to 390F.
- Mix all the seasoning together in a bowl.
- Toss the shrimp with the olive oil until it's well coated.
- Coat the shrimp with the spice mixture.
- Place the shrimp in your air fryer and allow them to cook for 5 minutes.
- Serve the cooked shrimp with the side of your choice.

Crispy Coconut Shrimp with Spicy Citrus Sauce

The shrimp has a lovely tropical flavor thanks to the coconut. The panko makes the shrimp nice and crispy. The spicy citrus sauce balances out and compliments the sweetness of the shrimp. They're perfect for your next party.

Prep Time: 10 Minutes / Cook Time: 20 Minutes / Servings: 2

Ingredients:
8 large organic shrimp, shelled and deveined
8 oz. coconut milk
1/2 cup shredded, sweetened coconut
1/2 cup panko bread crumbs
1/2 tsp. cayenne pepper
1/4 tsp. kosher salt
1/4 tsp. fresh ground pepper

Citrus Sauce:
1/2 cup orange marmalade
1 tbsp. honey
1 tsp. mustard
1/4 tsp. hot sauce

Cooking spray with olive oil

Directions:
- Spray the basket of your air fryer with cooking spray.
- Preheat your air fryer to 350F.
- Place the coconut milk in a bowl and season with the salt and pepper. Use a whisk to mix the ingredients.
- Place the shredded coconut in a different bowl with the panko, cayenne, and salt and pepper. Use a whisk to mix the ingredients together.
- Coat the shrimp with the coconut milk and then coat it with the panko mixture.

- Place the shrimp in your air fryer and cook for 20 minutes or a few minutes longer if not completely cooked.
- Place the sauce ingredient in a bowl and use a whisk to combine them, while the shrimp is cooking.
- Serve the cooked shrimp with a side of the spicy citrus sauce.

Sweet Citrus Salmon

The salmon has a nice mix of sweet and citrus, thanks to the sugar and lemon pepper. The yogurt sauce adds a little creaminess and freshness to give balance to the sweetness of the salmon. Serve the salmon with a side salad if you want to be healthy or fries if you want to splurge a little

Prep Time: 10 Minutes / Cook Time: 10 Minutes / Servings: 2

Ingredients:
8 oz. organic salmon filets, cut into 4 oz. portions
1/2 tsp. Lemon Pepper
1 tsp. dark brown sugar
2 dashes Extra Virgin Olive Oil

Sauce
1/4 cup plain low-fat yogurt Greek style is preferred
1/2 tsp. dill weed
1/4 tsp. garlic powder
1/2 tsp. lemon zest

2 sprigs Fresh dill, garnish
2 wedges lemon, garnish and squeeze onto salmon

Directions:
- Preheat your air fryer to 400F for at least 4 minutes.
- Season the salmon with the lemon pepper and sugar.
- Give the salmon a light coating of olive oil.
- Place the salmon in your air fryer and allow it to cook for 10 minutes.
- While the salmon is cooking, mix together the sauce ingredients in a medium sized bowl.
- Top the cooked salmon with a dollop of the sauce and then a sprig of fresh dill.
- Serve with a lemon wedge for squeezing and the side of your choice.

Soy Lemon Sugar Salmon

This salmon gives you a balance of 3 delicious flavors. The soy sauce gives you a nice salty savory flavor, the lemon juice gives you a fresh citrus flavor, and the sugar gives you the sweetness the brings everything together. The best part is you do very little work to enjoy this mouthwatering dish.

Prep Time: 2 Hours 10 Minutes / Cook Time: 8 Minutes / Servings: 2

Ingredients:
2, 8-oz. organic Salmon fillets
garlic powder, to taste
black pepper and salt, to taste

Marinade:
1/3 cup low-sodium soy sauce
1/3 cup light brown sugar
1/3 cup water
fresh squeezed lemon juice from 1 large lemon

2 tbsp. olive oil
scallion slices, garnish
cherry tomato, garnish

Directions:
- Rinse the salmon and use paper towels to pat it dry. Use salt, pepper, and garlic powder to season the salmon to your taste.
- Mix the marinade ingredients in a bowl. Add in the salmon, cover the bowl, and allow it to marinate in the refrigerator for a minimum of 2 hours.
- Preheat your air fryer to 355F.
- Put the marinated salmon in your air fryer and cook it for 8 minutes.
- Serve the cooked salmon with a garnish of sliced scallion and cherry tomato.

Crab Cake Sliders

Get ready to have delicious sliders in 15 minutes with this recipe. It takes only a few minutes to put together your crab slider patties that have delicious old bay taste, and great texture - thanks to the bell peppers. Then 10 minutes in the air fryer and you've got the fanciest sliders on the block!

Prep Time: 5 Minutes / Cook Time: 10 Minutes / Servings: 4

Ingredients:
8 oz. of organic jumbo lump crab meat
1/3 cup whole wheat bread crumbs
¼ cup red peppers, diced
¼ cup green peppers, diced
1 medium organic egg
¼ cup reduced fat mayo
½ tbsp. lemon juice
1 tsp. whole wheat flour
1 tbsp. Old Bay Seasoning
cooking oil with olive oil
whole wheat slider buns

Directions:
- Preheat your air fryer to 375F.
- Place all the ingredients except for the cooking oil, buns and flour in a bowl. Mix them together until well combined.
- Make the mixture into 8 slider sized patties. Sprinkle them with a little flour.
- Put the patties in your air fryer and give them a light spritz with the cooking oil. Allow the patties to cook for 10 minutes.
- Place the patties in the slider buns to serve.

Crab Fried Rice

Enjoy the luxurious taste of crab fried rice at home. You save a lot of money making this at home because you avoid the restaurant price mark up for crab. The dish comes out tasting like it was made at your favorite Chinese restaurant with very little work!

Prep Time: 10 Minutes / Cook Time: 20 Minutes / Servings: 6

Ingredients:
3 cups cold brown rice, cooked
1 cup frozen peas and carrots
6 tbsps. low-sodium soy sauce
1 tbsp. olive oil
1/2 cup onion, diced
1 cup organic lump crab meat
Cooking spray with olive oil

Directions:
- Preheat your air fryer to 360F.
- Put the rice in a bowl and mix in the oil and soy sauce. Make sure all ingredients are well mixed.
- Mix in the onions, crab, peas and carrots. Make sure all ingredients are well mixed again.
- Put the mixture in a non-stick pan that's small enough to fit in your air fryer. Or spray cooking in a pan small enough to fit in your air fryer before adding in the mixture.
- Put the pan into your air fryer and allow it cook for 20 minutes.
- Once it's cooked, place the rice in a bowl or on a plate to serve.

Lobster Tails with Lemon Garlic Butter

Lobster tails are one of the most delicious foods out there. We don't want to do much to their rich flavor, so we add a little lemon garlic butter. The lemon adds a little freshness while the garlic adds a nice aromatic taste to the rich lobster

Prep Time: 10 Minutes / Cook Time: 6 Minutes / Servings: 2

Ingredients:
4 organic lobster tails

Lemon Garlic Butter:
2 tbsp. organic butter
1 tbsp. Lemon Juice
Salt, to taste
Pepper, to taste
2 tsps. Minced garlic

Directions:
- Preheat your air fryer to 380F.
- Heat a small sauce pan on medium heat and add in the butter. Let the butter melt and add in the garlic. Let the garlic cook for about 30 seconds until it becomes fragrant. Take the butter of the heat and mix in the lemon juice and salt and pepper to taste.
- Use kitchen scissors to carefully cut open the lobster tails. Then carefully break and pull back the shell to expose the meat.
- Brush the lobster tails with the lemon garlic butter.
- Put the lobster in your air fryer and cook them for 4 minutes. After the 4 minutes, brush the lobster with any leftover lemon garlic butter and cook for 2 additional minutes.
- Serve with a side dish of your choice.

Keto Friendly Shrimp Scampi

Shrimp scampi has such an amazing rich flavor. The shrimp has a lovely buttery, citrusy, and slightly spicy flavor. This is balanced by the freshness of the chives and the aromatic flavor of the basil. The chicken broth brings depth to the dish.

Prep Time: 2 Hours 10 Minutes / Cook Time: 8 Minutes / Servings: 2

Ingredients:
4 tbsps. organic butter
1 tbsp. lemon juice
1 tbsp. minced garlic
2 tsps. red pepper flakes
1 tbsp. chopped chives or 1 tsp. dried chives
1 tbsp. minced basil leaves plus more for sprinkling or 1 tsp. dried basil
2 tbsp. chicken stock or white wine
1 lb. organic shrimp, peeled and deveined

Directions:
- Set your air fryer to 330F. Put a 6x3 metal pan in the basket before it heats up.
- Once the air fryer reaches 330F, add the red pepper, butter, and garlic to the metal pan.
- Allow the mixture to cook for 2 minutes, making sure to stir the mixture once during the cooking process.
- Add in the chives, then basil, then stock or wine, and finally the shrimp. Cook the mixture for 5 minutes, making sure to stir the mixture once during the cooking process.
- Allow the cooked mixture to rest for 1 minute before stirring again.
- Top with more basil for garnish and serve.

Bacon Wrapped Scallops

The combination of bacon and scallops is perfect. You get the saltiness of the bacon paired with the delicate flavor of the scallops. The lemon pepper adds a little light citrusy flavor and the paprika adds a hint of sweetness

Prep Time: 20 Minutes / Cook Time: 6 Minutes / Servings: 4

Ingredients:
20 Raw organic Sea Scallops,
5 slices organic Center-Cut Bacon
1 tsp. lemon pepper seasoning
1 tsp. Paprika
Cooking Spray with olive oil
20 toothpicks

Directions:
- Preheat your air fryer to 400F.
- Spray the basket with cooking spray.
- Rinse the scallops and lay them between 2 paper towels to dry and absorb any excess moisture.
- Cut every slice of bacon into 4 equal sized pieces.
- Wrap 1 of the smaller pieces of bacon around 1 of the scallops and use a toothpick to hold it in place. Repeat with the remaining scallops and bacon.
- Season both sides of the exposed scallop with paprika and lemon pepper.
- Place the scallops in your air fryer and give them a light mist of cooking spray and cook for 5-6 minutes.
- Remove the toothpicks from the cooked scallops and serve.

Sarah Conner

Sides

Asparagus with Basil & Olive Oil

This a quick and easy way to make perfect asparagus. The basil gives the asparagus distinctive flavor. This works well as a side for steak or chicken.

Prep Time: 5 Minutes / Cook Time: 10 Minutes / Servings: 2

Ingredients:
½ bunch asparagus
1 tsp. basil
Salt, to taste
Avocado or olive oil in a spray bottle

Directions:
> Trim the ends of your asparagus.
> Put the asparagus in the basket of your air fryer and lightly spray it with the oil then sprinkle the basil on. Season with salt for taste.
> Put the basket back in your air fryer and cook for 10 minutes at 400F.
> Serve with a protein of your choice.

Asparagus with Lemon Pepper

This a quick and easy way to make perfect asparagus. The lemon pepper gives the asparagus a little citrus flavor which pairs well with the fresh light flavor of the asparagus. This works well as a side of steak or chicken

Prep Time: 5 Minutes / Cook Time: 10 Minutes / Servings: 2

Ingredients:
½ bunch asparagus
Lemon pepper, to taste
Salt, to taste
Avocado or olive oil in a spray bottle

Directions:
- Trim the ends of your asparagus.
- Put the asparagus in the basket of your air fryer and lightly spray it with the oil. Season with lemon pepper and salt to taste.
- Put the basket back in your air fryer and cook for 10 minutes at 400F.
- Serve with the protein of your choice.

Asparagus with Carrots

This asparagus and carrot combination is a great side dish that pairs with any meal you can think of. Fish, steak, pork or chicken. It even goes with any vegetarian dish

Prep Time: 5 Minutes / Cook Time: 10 Minutes / Servings: 2

Ingredients:
½ bunch asparagus
3 full carrots
Salt to, taste
Avocado or olive oil in a spray bottle

Directions:
- Trim the ends of your asparagus and cut the carrots into strips as thin as the asparagus.
- Put the asparagus and carrots in the basket of your air fryer and lightly spray it with the oil. Season with salt for taste.
- Put the basket back in your air fryer and cook for 10 minutes at 400F.
- Serve immediately.

Honey Carrots

These carrots are oh, so sweet and satisfying. The natural sweetness of the carrots comes out when they're cooked and is only intensified by the addition of honey. The salt and pepper balance out the sweetness of the carrots with honey. These are great as a side dish for turkey.

Prep Time: 5 Minutes / Cook Time: 10 Minutes / Servings: 2

Ingredients:
3 cups of carrots, cut into large pieces
1 tbsp. Olive oil
1 tbsp. Honey
Salt and pepper, to taste

Directions:
- Preheat your air fryer to 200F.
- Mix the carrots, honey and olive oil together in a bowl until carrots are completely covered.
- Season the carrots with salt and pepper for taste.
- Put the carrots in your air fryer and allow them to cook for 12 minutes.
- Serve immediately.

Asian Style Cauliflower and Carrots

There is something great about adding soy sauce to vegetables. It gives a great flavor to the carrots and cauliflower. It makes the dish delicious and it can pair with any meal...

Prep Time: 5 Minutes / Cook Time: 10 Minutes / Servings: 2

Ingredients:
3 cups of carrots, cut into large pieces
½ bouquet of cauliflower
1 tbsp. Olive oil
1 tbsp. low-sodium Soy Sauce
Pepper, to taste

Directions:
- Preheat your air fryer to 200F.
- Mix the carrots, cauliflower, soy sauce and olive oil together in a bowl until vegetables are completely covered.
- Put the vegetables in your air fryer and allow them to cook for 12 minutes.
- Season the vegetables with pepper for taste.
- Serve immediately.

Non-Fried Pickles

Fried pickles are incredibly delicious. You get the breaded crunch on the outside and the soft, tangy, salty, pickle taste on the inside. These things are addictive, which isn't a problem because they're not fried. Serve with a side of ranch for dipping if you want even more flavor.

Prep Time: 10 Minutes / Cook Time: 10 Minutes / Servings: 2

Ingredients:
2 cups dill pickle slices
1 organic egg, whisked with 1 tbsp. water
3/4 cup panko breadcrumbs
1/4 cup freshly grated fat-free parmesan
1 tsp. dried oregano
Light Ranch, for dipping
Cooking spray with olive oil

Directions:
- Spray the basket of your air fryer with cooking spray.
- Preheat your air fryer to 360F.
- Pat the pickles dry using a paper towel.
- Mix together the parmesan, oregano and breadcrumbs in bowl until well combined.
- Coat the pickles with the egg mixture and then the parmesan breadcrumb mixture.
- Place the pickles in your air fryer and cook for 10 minutes flipping halfway through.
- Serve immediately with a side of ranch.

Garlic Non-Fried Pickles

Fried pickles with garlic...are you kidding me? You will lose your mind when eating these delicious and tasty tidbits. Serve with a side of ranch for dipping if you want even more flavor.

Prep Time: 10 Minutes / Cook Time: 10 Minutes / Servings: 2

Ingredients:
2 cups dill pickle slices
1 organic egg, whisked with 1 tbsp. water
3/4 cup panko breadcrumbs
1/4 cup freshly grated fat-free parmesan
1 tsp. dried oregano
1 tsp. garlic powder
Light Ranch or honey mustard, for dipping
Cooking spray with olive oil

Directions:
- Spray the basket of your air fryer with cooking spray.
- Preheat your air fryer to 360F.
- Pat the pickles dry using a paper towel.
- Mix together the parmesan, oregano, breadcrumbs, and garlic powder in bowl until well combined.
- Coat the pickles with the egg mixture and then the parmesan breadcrumb mixture
- Place the pickles in your air fryer and cook for 10 minutes flipping halfway through.
- Serve immediately with a side of ranch.

Spicy Non-Fried Pickles

Fried pickles are incredibly delicious. You get the breaded crunch on the outside and the soft, spicy, salty, pickle taste on the inside. These things are addictive which isn't a problem because they're not fried. Serve with a side of ranch for dipping if you want even more flavor.

Prep Time: 10 Minutes / Cook Time: 10 Minutes / Servings: 2

Ingredients:
2 cups dill pickle slices
1 organic egg, whisked with 1 tbsp. water
3/4 cup panko breadcrumbs
1/4 cup freshly grated fat-free parmesan
1 tsp. dried oregano
1 tsp. garlic powder
¼ tsp. cayenne pepper
Light Ranch, for dipping
Cooking spray with olive oil

Directions:
- Spray the basket of your air fryer with cooking spray.
- Preheat your air fryer to 360F.
- Pat the pickles dry using a paper towel.
- Mix together the parmesan, oregano, breadcrumbs, cayenne pepper and garlic powder in bowl until well combined.
- Coat the pickles with the egg mixture and then the parmesan breadcrumb mixture.
- Place the pickles in your air fryer and cook for 10 minutes flipping halfway through.
- Serve immediately with a side of ranch.

Golden Crisp French Fries

French fries are delicious for any occasion. Crispy golden-brown fries will put a smile on anyone's face at any moment in time. Simply delicious.

Prep Time: 10 Minutes / Cook Time: 10 Minutes / Servings: 4

Ingredients:
2 medium peeled red potatoes, about 12 ounces total weight
2 tsps. olive oil
1/2 tsp kosher salt
fresh black pepper, to taste

Directions:
- Preheat your air fryer to 400F for at least 8 minutes.
- Spray the basket of your air fryer with a little oil.
- Cut the potatoes into ¼ inch thick sticks.
- Place the 2 teaspoons of oil and spices in a bowl and mix them together. Add in the potatoes and toss until well coated.
- Place the potatoes in your air fryer in a few batches. Cook each batch for 8 – 10 minutes flipping the fries over halfway through.
- Serve immediately with a protein of your choice. Or enjoy them on their own with some ketchup or BBQ sauce.

Golden Scallion Garlic Fries

Garlic fries are delicious and a treat that is hard to beat. Remember the saying..." There's never enough garlic!" Enjoy

Prep Time: 10 Minutes / Cook Time: 10 Minutes / Servings: 4

Ingredients:
2 medium peeled red potatoes, about 12 ounces total weight
2 tsps. olive oil
1 tbsp. finely chopped scallions
2 tbsps. minced garlic
1/2 tsp. kosher salt
fresh black pepper, to taste

Directions:
- Preheat your air fryer to 400F for at least 8 minutes.
- Spray the basket of your air fryer with a little oil.
- Cut the potatoes into ¼ inch thick sticks.
- Place the 2 teaspoons of oil and spices in a bowl and mix them together. Add in the potatoes and toss until well coated.
- Place the potatoes in your air fryer in a few batches. Cook each batch for 8 – 10 minutes flipping the fries over halfway through.
- Serve immediately with a protein of your choice. Or enjoy them on their own with some ketchup or BBQ sauce.

Parmesan Fries

These parmesan fries are something that your family and friends will be talking about for a long time. They will love you for this tasty treat!

Prep Time: 10 Minutes / Cook Time: 10 Minutes / Servings: 4

Ingredients:
2 medium peeled red potatoes, about 12 ounces total weight
2 tsps. olive oil
1 tbsp. finely chopped scallions
1 cup fat-free Parmesan cheese
1/2 tsp. kosher salt
fresh black pepper, to taste

Directions:
- Preheat your air fryer to 400F for at least 8 minutes.
- Spray the basket of your air fryer with a little oil.
- Cut the potatoes into ¼ inch thick sticks.
- Place the 2 teaspoons of oil and spices in a bowl and mix them together. Add in the potatoes and toss until well coated.
- Place the potatoes in your air fryer in a few batches. Cook each batch for 8 – 10 minutes flipping the fries over halfway through.
- When done, take 1 light spray of oil over the hot fries then sprinkle the parmesan cheese over the top of the fries in abundance!
- Serve immediately with a protein of your choice. Or enjoy them on their own with some ketchup or BBQ sauce.

Garlic Parmesan Fries

The garlic infused with parmesan cheese makes these fries almost like a delicious meal in itself! Try this one and you will hit a home run! Enjoy

Prep Time: 10 Minutes / Cook Time: 10 Minutes / Servings: 4

Ingredients:
2 medium peeled red potatoes, about 12 ounces total weight
2 tsps. olive oil
1 tbsp. finely chopped scallions
1 cup fat-free Parmesan cheese
2 tbsp. minced garlic
1/2 tsp. kosher salt
fresh black pepper, to taste

Directions:
- Preheat your air fryer to 400F for at least 8 minutes.
- Spray the basket of your air fryer with a little oil.
- Cut the potatoes into ¼ inch thick sticks.
- Place the 2 teaspoons of oil and spices in a bowl and mix them together. Add in the potatoes and toss until well coated.
- Place the potatoes in your air fryer in a few batches. Cook each batch for 8 – 10 minutes flipping the fries over halfway through.
- When done, take 1 light spray of oil over the hot fries then sprinkle the parmesan cheese over the top of the fries in abundance!
- Serve immediately with a protein of your choice. Or enjoy them on their own with some ketchup or BBQ sauce.

Garlic Parmesan Jalapeño Fries

The garlic infused with parmesan cheese and jalapeno makes these fries almost like a delicious meal in itself! Try this one and you will hit a home run! Enjoy

Prep Time: 10 Minutes / Cook Time: 10 Minutes / Servings: 4

Ingredients:
2 medium peeled red potatoes, about 12 ounces total weight
2 tsps. olive oil
2 jalapeno peppers, diced
1 tbsp. scallions, finely chopped
1 cup fat-free Parmesan cheese
2 tbsps. minced garlic
1/2 tsp. kosher salt
fresh black pepper, to taste

Directions:
- Preheat your air fryer to 400F for at least 8 minutes.
- Spray the basket of your air fryer with a little oil.
- Cut the potatoes into ¼ inch thick sticks.
- Place the 2 teaspoons of oil and spices in a bowl and mix them together. Add in the potatoes and toss until well coated.
- Place the potatoes in your air fryer in a few batches. Cook each batch for 8 – 10 minutes flipping the fries over halfway through.
- When done, dump the fries into a large bowl. Take 1 light spray of oil over the hot crisp fries. Add the garlic, jalapeños and parmesan cheese over the top of the fries. Toss well and serve hot!

Sweet Potato Fries

These fries make a delicious healthy side dish. Sweet potatoes are packed with vitamins and are a good source of energy. These fries are a staple on any kitchen table.

Prep Time: 10 Minutes / Cook Time: 10 Minutes / Servings: 4

Ingredients:
2 medium peeled sweet potatoes, about 12 ounces total weight
2 tsps. olive oil
1/2 tsp kosher salt
1/4 tsp. sweet paprika
fresh black pepper, to taste

Directions:
- Preheat your air fryer to 400F for at least 8 minutes.
- Spray the basket of your air fryer with a little oil.
- Cut the sweet potatoes into ¼ inch thick sticks.
- Place the 2 teaspoons of oil and spices in a bowl and mix them together. Add in the sweet potatoes and toss until well coated.
- Place the sweet potatoes in your air fryer in a few batches. Cook each batch for 8 minutes flipping the fries over halfway through.
- Serve immediately with a protein of your choice. Or enjoy them on their own with some ketchup or BBQ sauce.

Spicy Sweet Potato Fries

These fries make a delicious healthy side dish. Sweet potatoes are packed with vitamins and are a good source of energy. The spiciness of the cayenne is matched by the sweetness of the paprika and sweet potatoes.

Prep Time: 10 Minutes / Cook Time: 10 Minutes / Servings: 4

Ingredients:
2 medium peeled sweet potatoes, about 12 ounces total weight
2 tsps. olive oil
1/2 tsp. kosher salt
1/2 tsp. garlic powder
1/4 tsp. sweet paprika
¼ tsp. cayenne pepper
fresh black pepper, to taste

Directions:
- Preheat your air fryer to 400F for at least 8 minutes.
- Spray the basket of your air fryer with a little oil.
- Cut the sweet potatoes into ¼ inch thick sticks.
- Place the 2 teaspoons of oil and spices in a bowl and mix them together. Add in the sweet potatoes and toss until well coated.
- Place the sweet potatoes in your air fryer in a few batches. Cook each batch for 8 minutes flipping the fries over halfway through.
- Serve immediately with a protein of your choice. Or enjoy them on their own with some ketchup or BBQ sauce.

Sarah Conner

Truffle Parmesan Fries

These fries make a delicious healthy side dish. Sweet potatoes are packed with vitamins and are a good source of energy. The spiciness of the cayenne is matched by the sweetness of the paprika and sweet potatoes. And, when we add a little truffle, we make this dish something to remember.

Prep Time: 10 Minutes / Cook Time: 10 Minutes / Servings: 2

Ingredients:
3 medium russet potatoes
2 tbsps. fat-free parmesan cheese
2 tbsps. finely chopped fresh parsley
1 tbsp. olive oil
Truffle salt, to taste
Cooking spray with olive oil

Directions:
- Preheat your air fryer to 360F for at least 3 minutes.
- Spray the basket of your air fryer with cooking spray.
- Cut the potatoes into ¼ inch thick sticks.
- Use a paper towel to pat the potatoes dry.
- Place the f oil and spices in a bowl and mix them together. Add in the potatoes and toss until well coated.
- Place the potatoes in your air fryer and cook for 20 minutes. Flip the fries at the 10-minute mark and again at the 15-minute mark.
- Serve immediately.

Garlic Parmesan Roasted Potatoes

Garlic and parmesan are always a winning combo. The parmesan gives the potatoes some salty cheesy goodness, and the garlic adds a savory aromatic flavor. They mix well together with the creamy flavor of the potatoes. These make a great side dish for any type of meat or fish.

Prep Time: 10 Minutes / Cook Time: 20 Minutes / Servings: 6

Ingredients:
½ tsp. dried basil
5 cloves garlic, minced
½ tsp. dried oregano,
2 tbsps. parsley leaves
3 lbs. red potatoes
1 tsp. dried thyme
Kosher salt, to taste
freshly ground black pepper, to taste
2 tbsps. olive oil
2 tbsps. organic butter, unsalted and melted
⅓ cup grated fat-free Parmesan cheese
1 sheet of baking paper

Directions:
- Put a sheet of baking paper in the basket of your air fryer.
- Preheat your air fryer to 400F.
- Wash the potatoes and pat them dry with paper towels.
- Slice the potatoes into quarters.
- Put all the ingredients into a bowl and mix well.
- Add in the potatoes and toss until well coated.
- Put the potatoes in your air fryer and allow them to cook for 18-20 minutes. Flip the potatoes after 10 minutes.
- Serve immediately.

Turmeric Tofu and Cauliflower Rice

This is a healthy vegan side dish that everyone will love. Cauliflower rice is one of the latest health crazes out there. Here you're substituting vitamin packed cauliflower for regular rice. You can find cauliflower rice at many markets or you can make it by pulsing cauliflower in a food processor or blender until it becomes the size of a grain of rice.

Prep Time: 10 Minutes / Cook Time: 20 Minutes / Servings: 6

Ingredients:
Tofu:
1/2 block firm or extra firm tofu
2 tbsps. low-sodium soy sauce
1/2 cup onion, diced
1 cup carrots, diced
1 tsp. turmeric

Cauliflower Rice:
3 cups cauliflower rice
2 tbsps. low-sodium soy sauce
1 1/2 tsps. toasted sesame oil optional,
1 tbsp. rice vinegar
1 tbsp. minced ginger
1/2 cup finely chopped broccoli
2 cloves garlic, minced
1/2 cup frozen peas

Directions:
- Preheat your air fryer to 370F.
- Crumble the tofu into small pieces into a bug bowl. Add in the remaining tofu ingredients and mix well.
- Place the mixture in your air fryer and cook for 10 minutes. Shake the mixture halfway through.
- While the tofu mixture is cooking, place the cauliflower rice ingredients in the bowl you mixed the tofu in. Mix the ingredients together until they're well combined.

- Place the cooked tofu ingredients in a serving bowl and set aside.
- Place the cauliflower rice ingredients in your air fryer and cook for 10 minutes. Shake the mixture halfway through. If the rice isn't cooked through after 10 minutes cook for an additional 2-5 minutes.
- Place the cooked rice in the bowl with the tofu and toss until well combined.
- Serve immediately.

Fried Ravioli with Marinara Sauce

Fried ravioli is an incredible delicious side dish or appetizer. You get the crunchy outside from the breading and then are rewarded with a hot melted cheese center. Combine them with some marinara sauce and its pure heaven. The biggest drawback is the fact that they're fried. You get to bypass that drawback when you make a healthier version in your air fryer.

Prep Time: 10 Minutes / Cook Time: 5 Minutes / Servings: 6

Ingredients:
1, 14-ounce jar marinara sauce
1, 9-ounce box fat-free cheese ravioli or meat ravioli, store-bought
1 tsp. olive oil
2 cups low-sodium Italian-style bread crumbs
1 cup low-fat buttermilk
¼ cup fat-free Parmesan cheese
1 sheet of baking paper

Directions:
- Put a sheet of baking paper in the basket of your air fryer.
- Preheat your air fryer to 200F.
- Put the breadcrumbs and olive oil in a bowl and mix them together. Place the buttermilk in a bowl.
- Dip the ravioli in the buttermilk and then coat them with the breadcrumb mixture.
- Place the ravioli in your air fryer and cook for 5 minutes.
- While the ravioli is cooking, heat up some marinara sauce in the stove or in the microwave.
- Serve the ravioli with a side of the marinara.

Avocado Fries with Lime Dip

Avocado fries are probably something you've never heard of, but you're going to be so glad you did. They're crunchy on the outside and creamy on the inside. They have a wonderful chili lime flavor, thanks to the seasoning. The lime dip is so creamy and helps to combat the heat from the chili. It's a delicious now way to eat avocado!

Prep Time: 10 Minutes / Cook Time: 8 Minutes / Servings: 2

Ingredients:
Avocado Fries:
8 oz. (2 small) avocados, peeled, pitted and cut into 16 wedges
1 large organic egg, lightly beaten
3/4 cup panko breadcrumbs
1 1/4 tsps. lime chili seasoning salt, like Tajin Classic

Lime Dipping Sauce:
1/4 cup Greek Yogurt
3 tbsps. light mayonnaise
2 tsps. fresh lime juice
1/2 tsp. lime chili seasoning salt, such as Tajin Classic
1/8 tsp. kosher salt

Cooking Spray with olive oil

Directions:
- Spray the basket of your air fryer with cooking spray.
- Preheat your air fryer to 390F.
- Mix together the panko and lime chili seasoning in a bowl. Place the egg in a small bowl.
- Coat the avocado with the egg and then with the panko mixture.
- Place the avocado fries in your air fryer and cook for 7-8 minutes. Flip the fries halfway through the cooking process.
- While the avocado fries are cooking, Place all the lime dip ingredients in a bowl. Mix them together until well combined.
- Serve the fries immediately with the lime dipping sauce.

Stuffed Mushrooms

Stuffed mushrooms are perfect for any event. The mushrooms are nice and soft on the outside and crunchy in the middle, thanks to the breadcrumbs. The seasoning salt gives the mushrooms a lovely tangy flavor.

Prep Time: 10 Minutes / Cook Time: 8 Minutes / Servings: 2

Ingredients:
10 oz. fresh white mushrooms
1 cup whole wheat flour
½ cup cornstarch
¾ cup baking powder
1 tsp. seasoning salt
1 cup water
2 cups panko breadcrumbs

Cooking Spray with olive oil

Directions:
- Spray the basket of your air fryer with cooking spray.
- Preheat your air fryer to 360F.
- Wipe off the mushrooms to make sure they're clean.
- In a bowl, combine the cornstarch, salt, baking powder, and flour. Make sure they're well mixed. Pour in the water and stir to combine everything. Place the panko in a separate bowl.
- Coat the mushrooms with the cornstarch mixture and then coat it with the panko.
- Place the mushrooms in your air fryer and cook them for 7 minutes. Make sure you shake the basket halfway through cooking.
- Serve immediately.

Honey Glazed Button Mushrooms

Honey glazed mushrooms are simply delicious. This is a dish that you can serve as a side dish for any occasion. And again, they are simply delicious.

Prep Time: 10 Minutes / Cook Time: 8 Minutes / Servings: 2

Ingredients:
12 oz. fresh white mushrooms
1 tsp. seasoning salt
1 tbsp. Dijon mustard
1 tsp. honey
Pepper, to taste
Cooking spray with olive oil

Directions:
- Spray the basket of your air fryer with cooking spray.
- Preheat your air fryer to 360F.
- Wipe off the mushrooms to make sure they're clean.
- Spray mushrooms with light oil.
- In a bowl, add mushrooms, pepper, seasoning salt and toss.
- Place the mushrooms in your air fryer and cook them for 5 minutes. Make sure you shake the basket halfway through cooking.
- Coat or brush the mushrooms with the Dijon/honey mixture.
- Place back into the air fryer for another 3 minutes.
- Serve immediately.

Zucchini Fries

This is a great way to get kids to eat they're vegetables. Kids will eat just about anything fried and yes you can get them to eat zucchini. You're happy knowing the food actually isn't fried and provides a good amount of nutrition. We serve it with a roasted garlic aioli, so the grown-ups can enjoy too!

Prep Time: 10 Minutes / Cook Time: 8 Minutes / Servings: 3

Ingredients:

Roasted Garlic Aioli:
1 tsp. roasted garlic
2 tbsp. olive oil
½ cup reduced fat mayonnaise
juice of ½ lemon
salt and pepper, to taste

Zucchini Fries:
½ cup whole wheat flour
2 organic eggs, beaten
1 cup low-sodium seasoned breadcrumbs
salt and pepper, to taste
1 large zucchini, cut into ½-inch sticks
olive oil in a spray bottle, can or mister

Directions:
- Put the flour in one bowl, the egg in another bowl, and the breadcrumbs and salt and pepper in a 3rd bowl.
- Dip the zucchini in the flour, then egg, and finally the seasoned bread crumbs.
- Let the zucchini rest for about 10 minutes.
- While the zucchini is resting, preheat your air fryer to 400F.
- Spray the fries lightly with the olive oil spray and put them in your air fryer. Cook the fries for 12 minutes, flipping them halfway through.

- While the zucchini is cooking, whisk together all the aioli ingredients together in a bowl, except for the salt and pepper. When they're well mixed, add salt and pepper for taste.
- Serve the zucchini fries with the aioli.

Shishido Peppers with Asiago Cheese

Shishido peppers have a lovely mild flavor that people that don't like spicy food will love. The peppers are topped with asiago cheese to give them some creaminess to balance out any heat you may encounter. They're a great side to serve just about any time of day.

Prep Time: 10 Minutes / Cook Time: 10 Minutes / Servings: 4

Ingredients:
6 oz. Shishido peppers
salt and pepper, to taste
1/2 tbsp. avocado oil
1/3 cups fat-free Asiago cheese, grated fine
Limes, for garnish

Directions:
- Clean the peppers by rinsing them with some water and using a paper towel to pat them dry.
- Preheat your air fryer to 350F.
- Put the oil in a bowl along with the peppers and toss until well coated. Season with salt and pepper to taste.
- Place the peppers in your air fryer and cook them for 10 minutes. Keep an eye on them during the last couple minutes so that they blister, but don't burn
- Squeeze lime juice on the cooked peppers and top with cheese to serve.

Salt & Vinegar Chips

Now you can make delicious chips at home without all the excess oil. These chips have a lovely mix of tangy and salty, thanks to the apple cider vinegar and salt. They're great on their own as a snack or as a side with a sandwich.

Prep Time: 25 Minutes / Cook Time: 12 Minutes Servings: 3

Ingredients:
5 baby yellow potatoes, thinly sliced
1 cup apple cider vinegar
½ tbsp. extra-virgin olive oil
½ tsp. sea salt

Directions:
- Place the apple cider vinegar and potatoes in the bowl. Mix them together and let them marinate together for 15 minutes.
- Preheat your air fryer to 360F.
- In a separate bowl mix together the remaining ingredients. Take the potatoes out of the vinegar and place them in this bowl. Toss together until the potatoes are well coated.
- Place the potatoes in your air fryer and cook for 12 minutes. Check the potatoes every 3 minutes to ensure they're cooking properly.
- Allow them to cool for a few minutes and serve.

Beet Chips

Beet chips have a lovely red color and a delicious earthy flavor. You can find them in a lot of store, but they're expensive. Save some money, make a healthy snack that doesn't require nearly as much oil as their store-bought counterpart. Serve them like you would regular chips/

Prep Time: 20 Minutes / Cook Time: 1 Hour 5 Minutes / Servings: 4

Ingredients:
3 medium-size red beets, peeled and cut into 1/8-inch thick slices (about 3 cups slices)
2 tsps. canola oil
3/4 tsp. kosher salt
1/4 tsp. black pepper

Directions:
> Slice the beets into 1/8-inch pieces using a knife or a mandolin if you have one.
> Preheat your air fryer to 320F.
> Place the beets in a bowl with the remaining ingredients and toss until the beats are well coated,
> Place the beats in your air fryer in 2 separate batches and cook each batch for 25-30 minutes. Make sure to shake the basket about every 5 minutes.
> Allow the chips to cool for a few minutes before serving.

Potato Chips

Potato chips have been around for centuries and making them in the convenience of your own home is a wonderful thing! Easy as 1-2-3! Enjoy!

Prep Time: 20 Minutes / Cook Time: 1 Hour 5 Minutes / Servings: 4

Ingredients:
3 medium-size Potatoes, peeled and cut into 1/8-inch thick slices (about 3 cups slices)
2 tsps. avocado oil
3/4 tsp. kosher salt
1/4 tsp. black pepper

Directions:
- Slice the potatoes into 1/8-inch pieces using a knife or a mandolin if you have one.
- Preheat your air fryer to 320F.
- Place the potatoes in a bowl with the remaining ingredients and toss until the potatoes are well coated,
- Place the potatoes in your air fryer in 2 separate batches and cook each batch for 25-30 minutes. Make sure to shake the basket about every 5 minutes.
- Allow the chips to cool for a few minutes before serving.

Parmesan Potato Chips

These Parmesan potato chips are a classic little appetizer for anyone to enjoy! Still easy to make but always want to share these tasty chips!

Prep Time: 20 Minutes / Cook Time: 1 Hour 5 Minutes / Servings: 4

Ingredients:
3 medium-size Potatoes, peeled and cut into 1/8-inch thick slices (about 3 cups slices)
2 tsps. avocado oil
2 tbsp. grated fat-free parmesan cheese
3/4 tsp. kosher salt
1/4 tsp. black pepper

Directions:
- Slice the potatoes into 1/8-inch pieces using a knife or a mandolin if you have one.
- Preheat your air fryer to 320F.
- Place the potatoes in a bowl with the remaining ingredients and toss until the potatoes are well coated,
- Place the potatoes in your air fryer in 2 separate batches and cook each batch for 25-30 minutes. Make sure to shake the basket about every 5 minutes.
- Toss the chips into a large bowl and sprinkle on the parmesan cheese.
- Allow the chips to cool for a few minutes before serving.

Garlic Parmesan Potato Chips

These Parmesan potato chips are a classic little appetizer for anyone to enjoy! Still easy to make but always want to share these tasty chips!

Prep Time: 20 Minutes / Cook Time: 1 Hour 5 Minutes / Servings: 4

Ingredients:
3 medium-size Potatoes, peeled and cut into 1/8-inch thick slices (about 3 cups slices)
1 tbsp. minced garlic
2 tsps. avocado oil
2 tbsps. grated fat-free parmesan cheese
3/4 tsp. kosher salt
1/4 tsp. black pepper

Directions:
- Slice the potatoes into 1/8-inch pieces using a knife or a mandolin if you have one.
- Preheat your air fryer to 320F.
- Place the potatoes in a bowl with the remaining ingredients and toss until the potatoes are well coated,
- Place the potatoes in your air fryer in 2 separate batches and cook each batch for 25-30 minutes. Make sure to shake the basket about every 5 minutes.
- Toss the chips into a large bowl and sprinkle on the parmesan cheese.
- Allow the chips to cool for a few minutes before serving.

Fried Green Tomatoes with Sriracha Mayonnaise Dipping Sauce

Fried green tomatoes are a delicious summer treat. They have a great crunchy fried exterior and a juicy, soft tomato interior. It's so easy to make them in your air fryer. You don't have to worry about how much oil you use to get the right consistency. The Sriracha mayo gives the tomatoes some creamy spiciness.

Prep Time: 15 Minutes / Cook Time: 16 Minutes / Servings: 4

Ingredients:
3 green tomatoes
Salt, to taste
freshly ground black pepper, to taste
⅓ cup whole wheat flour
2 organic eggs
½ cup low-fat buttermilk
1 cup panko breadcrumbs
1 cup cornmeal
fresh thyme sprigs or chopped fresh chives

Sriracha Mayo:
½ cup reduced-fat mayonnaise
2 tbsp. Sriracha hot sauce
1 tbsp. skim milk

Olive oil spray

Directions:
> Spray the olive oil spray in the basket of your air fryer
> Preheat your air fryer to 320F.
> Slice the tomatoes into ¼ inch pieces. Use a paper towel to pat them dry. Salt and pepper for taste.
> Put the flour in a small bowl, mix together the buttermilk and eggs in another, mix together the cornmeal and breadcrumbs in a 3rd bowl.

- Dip the tomatoes in the flour, then buttermilk mixture, and finally the cornmeal mixture.
- Place the tomatoes in your air fryer in batches of 3 or 4 and spray a little olive oil spray on top of the tomatoes. Cook for 8 minutes and flip the tomatoes halfway through spraying the tops again with olive oil spray. Repeat with remaining tomatoes.
- Mix together the Sriracha mayonnaise ingredients in a bowl while the tomatoes are cooking.
- Put the cooked tomatoes on a paper towel lined plate and allow them to cook for a few minutes.
- Serve the tomatoes with a side of the Sriracha mayonnaise.

Sarah Conner

Dessert

Apple Fries with Whip Cream Caramel Sauce

This is a delicious easy dessert to make. The apples warm up in the air fryer and get a little soft. The graham crackers give the apples a nice sweet crust. Dipping them into sauce makes it taste just like a caramel apple.

Prep Time: 15 Minutes / Cook Time: 15 Minutes / Servings: 6

Ingredients:
3 Pink Lady or Honeycrisp apples, peeled, cored and cut into 8 wedges
½ cup whole wheat flour
3 organic eggs, beaten
1 cup graham cracker crumbs
¼ cup sugar
8 oz. light whipped cream cheese
½ cup caramel sauce, plus more for garnish
Cooking spray with olive oil

Directions:
- Spray the basket of your air fryer with cooking spray.
- Preheat your air fryer to 380F. Place the eggs in a small bowl and mix the sugar and graham cracker in another small bowl.
- Place the apple slices in your air fryer in batches and cook for 7 minutes. Flip the apples after 5 minutes. Repeat the process with remaining apple slices.
- While the apples are cooking, mix together the cream cheese and caramel sauce in a bowl, until well combined. Make a fun design on top with more caramel sauce.
- Serve the cooked apples with the caramel sauce.

Peanut Butter and Banana Bites

These are incredible bite sized treats. The shell on the outside is crispy and crunchy, while the peanut butter and banana center is soft and gooey. They go great with vanilla ice cream and are really quick and easy to make.

Prep Time: 15 Minutes / Cook Time: 15 Minutes / Servings: 6

Ingredients:
1 large Banana (sliced)
12 Won Ton Wrappers
1/2 cup Peanut Butter
Olive oil spray

Directions:
- Preheat your air fryer to 380.
- Put water in a bowl and add a little lemon juice. Cut the banana in slices and place the slices in the water.
- Place 1 slice of banana in the center of one of the wonton wrappers. Top the banana slice with 1 teaspoon of peanut butter.
- Use a brush to coat the edges of the wonton with water. Bring 2 opposite sides of the wonton together and squeeze. Do the same with the remaining side. Repeat the process with the remaining banana slices.
- Place the wontons in your air fryer and spray with olive oil spray. Cook the bites for 6 minutes.
- Serve the bites with a side of vanilla ice cream.

Nutella and Banana Sandwiches

These are an easy and fast little dessert. The chocolaty nutty Nutella spread gets all gooey in the air fryer. This matches well with the soft bananas. The butter helps to make the sandwich crispy and adds a rich flavor.

Prep Time: 5 Minutes / Cook Time: 15 Minutes / Servings: 2

Ingredients:
Softened organic butter, enough for spread
4 slices whole wheat bread
¼ cup chocolate hazelnut spread (Nutella®)
1 banana

Directions:
- Preheat your air fryer to 370.
- Cut the banana into 6 pieces. Spread the Nutella on 1 side of each piece of bread. Place 3 pieces of banana on top of the Nutella on 2 pieces of bread. Top with the Nutella side of the remaining bread. Spread the butter on the other side of all 4 pieces of bread. Cut the sandwiches in half.
- Place the sandwiches in your air fryer and cook for 8 minutes. Flip the sandwiches after 5 minutes.
- Serve the hot sandwiches immediately with a glass of milk.

Double Chocolate Brownies

There's not too much work that goes into these delicious brownies. They come out oh so chocolatey, thanks to the chocolate chips. You can always swap out the chocolate chips for something else if you'd prefer nuts, carob chips, peanut butter chips, etc.

Prep Time: 10 Minutes / Cook Time: 20 Minutes / Servings: 4

Ingredients:

DRY INGREDIENTS:
1/2 cup whole wheat pastry flour
1/2 cup sugar
1/4 cup cocoa powder
1 tbsp. ground flax seeds
1/4 tsp. salt

WET INGREDIENTS:
1/4 cup non-dairy milk
1/4 cup aquafaba
1/2 tsp. vanilla extract

MIX-INS:
1/4 cup chocolate chips or mix-in of your choice
Cooking spray with olive oil

Directions:
- Preheat your air fryer to 350.
- Combine the wet ingredients together in a small bowl. Combine the dry ingredients together in a medium bowl.
- Pour the wet ingredients into the dry ingredient and combine well. Pour in the mix-ins and combine again.
- Spray a 6-inch round pie or cake pan with cooking spray and pour the mixture into it.
- Put the pan in your air fryer and cook for 20 minutes. If the center is not fully cooked after 20 minutes, cook for an additional 5 minutes.

- Allow the brownies to cool for a few minutes before serving

Popcorn

You don't have to go to the movies to get this one anymore. Movie popcorn was just so good, but now you can make it in the comfort of your own home! ;)

Prep Time: 5 Minutes / Cook Time: 15 Minutes / Servings: 6

Ingredients:
3 tbsps. dried corn kernels
spray avocado oil
salt, to taste

Directions:
- Line the sides of the air fryer basket with aluminum foil and preheat your air fryer to 390F.
- Place the corn kernels in the basket of your preheated air fryer, spray them with the oil and set the timer for 15 minutes. Stay close because the popcorn could finish sooner. If the popping sound stops the popcorn is cooked.
- Place the popcorn in a big bowl, spray with a little more oil, and add salt and for taste.
- Serve immediately.

Caramel Popcorn

There's no telling how many of these buckets you will be eating while you watch movies all evening. Great tasting with a sweet tooth in mind!

Prep Time: 5 Minutes / Cook Time: 15 Minutes / Servings: 6

Ingredients:
3 tbsps. dried corn kernels
spray avocado oil
salt, to taste

Caramel:
1/2 Cup Organic Sweet Butter Cream, Salted
1/2 Cup Light Brown Sugar
1 tsp. Vanilla
1/4 tsp. Baking Soda

Directions:
- Line the sides of the air fryer basket with aluminum foil and preheat your air fryer to 390F. Line a baking sheet with aluminum foil
- Place the corn kernels in the basket of your preheated air fryer, spray them with the oil and set the timer for 15 minutes. Stay close because the popcorn could finish sooner. If the popping sound stops the popcorn is cooked.
- Place the popcorn in a big bowl and salt for taste.
- Place the butter in a medium saucepan and heat it on medium heat until it melts.
- Mix in the brown sugar
- Keep stirring the mixture as it comes to a boil.
- Stop stirring the boiling mixture and let it cook for 5 minutes.
- After 4 minutes add the vanilla and stir. After the 5 minutes it's done add the baking soda.
- Pour the caramel sauce over the popcorn and use a spoon to combine the mixture until the popcorn is coated with caramel.
- Let the caramel corn on the aluminum foil lined baking sheet to cool
- Serve the popcorn once it's cooled.

Apple Dumplings

This homemade delight is a dessert from the past that should always be on the menu. You just can't say no to apple dumplings! Yummm!

Prep Time: 15 Minutes / Cook Time: 25 Minutes / Servings: 2

Ingredients:
2 very small apples, cored and peeled
2 tbsp. raisins or sultanas
1 tbsp. light brown sugar
2 sheets puff pastry
2 tbsp. organic butter, melted

Directions:
- Preheat your air fryer to 356F.
- Combine the brown sugar and sultanas or raisins in a bowl.
- Place each apple on a puff pastry sheet. Put some of the brown sugar mixture in the area where the core was in each apple.
- Fold the pastry up over the apple and cover it completely.
- Use a brush to coat the pastry with melted butter.
- Place aluminum foil in the basket of your preheated air fryer, place the pastries on top of it, and set the timer for 25 minutes. Flip the pastries about halfway through.
- Allow the cooked dumplings to cool for about 10 minutes before serving.

Fruit Crumble Mug Cake

When we tried this one we couldn't believe it! Wonderful fruit cake with a crumble. It is as sweet as it gets! You will be making cakes for a long time to come!

Prep Time: 15 Minutes / Cook Time: 15 Minutes / Servings: 4

Ingredients:
4 oz. whole wheat Flour
1/4 cup organic Butter
1/8 cup Sugar
1/8 cup Gluten Free Oats
2 tbsps. Light Brown Sugar
4 Plums
1 Small Apple
1 Small Pear
1 Small Peach
Handful of Blueberries
1 tbsp. Honey

Directions:
- Preheat your air fryer to 320F.
- Take out the stones and cores from all of the fruit. Slice the fruit in small square chunks.
- Divide the fruit between 4 mugs. Top with enough honey and brown sugar to cover the fruit.
- Mix the butter, sugar, and flour in a bowl until the mixture looks like small breadcrumbs. Then mix in the oats.
- Place the mixture on top of the fruit in each mug.
- Place the mugs in the basket of your preheated air fryer and set the timer for 10 minutes. After the ten minutes are up, raise the temperature to 390F and cook for an additional 5 minutes.
- Serve immediately.

Chocolate Cake

Chocolate has been one of the most requested desserts on the planet for years! We have one of the best chocolate cakes and its made right in your air fryer! Finger licking deliciousness.

Prep Time: 10 Minutes / Cook Time: 45 Minutes / Servings: 6-8

Ingredients:
¾ cup light Brown Sugar
½ whole wheat Flour
4 tbsps. Unsweetened Cocoa Powder
3/4 tsp. Baking Powder
3/4 tsp. Baking Soda
1/2 tsp. Salt
1 Large organic Egg
1/2 cup skim Milk
1/4 cup olive Oil
1 tsp. Vanilla Extract
1/2 cup Hot Water

Directions:
- Preheat your air fryer to 350F.
- Mix the first 6 ingredients in a large bowl. Then pour in the olive oil, milk, egg, and vanilla and mix well. Pour in the hot water and mix again.
- Let the mixture sit for 4 minutes.
- Coat an air fryer safe pan with cooking spray.
- Pour the batter into the pan and cover the top of the pan with aluminum foil. Poke holes in the foil.
- Place the pan in the basket of your preheated air fryer lower the temperature to 320F and set the timer for 35 minutes. After the 35 minutes, take the foil off the pan and cook for 10 more minutes. A toothpick placed in the center of the cake should come out clean when cooked.
- Let the cake cool for 10 minutes before serving.

Baked Apple

If you didn't think you could bake an apple, think again! Baked fruit is one of the best things you can do as a healthy treat! All you will say about this one is, "Make more please!"

Prep Time: 10 Minutes / Cook Time: 20 Minutes / Servings: 1

Ingredients:
1 medium apple
2 tbsps. chopped walnuts
2 tbsps. raisins
1 ½ tsps. organic butter, melted
¼ tsp. cinnamon
¼ tsp. nutmeg
¼ cup water

Directions:
- Preheat your air fryer to 355F.
- Slice the apple in half crosswise. Use a spoon to scoop out some of the inside.
- Mix the cinnamon, nutmeg, butter, raisins, and walnuts in a bowl.
- Spoon the mixture into the middle of the apple.
- Place the apple in an air fryer safe pan. Put the water in the pan.
- Place the pan in the basket of your preheated air fryer and set the timer for 20.
- Serve immediately with some vanilla ice cream.

Shortbread Cookies

Shortbread cookies are on the baking menu and your tummy is the final destination for them. Oh, so yummy in my tummy!

Prep Time: 10 Minutes / Cook Time: 20 Minutes / Servings: 2

Ingredients:
1 ½ cups whole wheat Flour
1/3 cup Sugar
¾ cup organic Butter
1 tsp. Vanilla Essence
Chocolate Chips, to mix in

Directions:
- Preheat your air fryer to 355F.
- Place all the ingredients except for the chocolate chips in a big bowl and mix until a dough forms.
- Roll the dough out and use a cookie cutter to create whatever shapes you'd like.
- Place the cookies in an air fryer safe baking tray.
- Place the dish in the basket of your preheated air fryer and set the timer for 10 minutes.
- After the 10 minutes, lower the temperature to 320, place the chocolate chips on top of the cookies, and bake for 10 more minutes.
- Allow the cookies to cool for a few minutes before serving.

Fried Banana S'more

If you've never had fried bananas, then having one on a S'more is the perfect way to break this one in for the first time. Easy to make and delicious.

Prep Time: 5 Minutes / Cook Time: 6 Minutes / Servings: 4

Ingredients:
4 bananas
3 tbsps. mini semi-sweet chocolate chips
3 tbsps. mini peanut butter chips
3 tbsps. mini marshmallows
3 tbsps. graham cracker cereal

Directions:
- Preheat your air fryer to 400F.
- Slice the banana with the peels still on in half lengthwise, but don't cut down through the bottom peel and don't cut through the ends. Open the banana a little so that you have a pocket for the other ingredients.
- Fill the pocket with the remaining ingredients.
- Place the bananas in the basket of your preheated air fryer with the filling side up and set the timer for 6 minutes. The banana is cooked when the chocolate melts, the peel turns black, and the banana is soft.
- Allow the bananas to cool for a few minutes before serving.

Mini Apple Pies

When's the last time you had a mini apple pie! It used to be the only thing you grabbed at the store if you had a hearty sweet tooth. Now you can make it right at home! Enjoy

Prep Time: 10 Minutes / Cook Time: 18 Minutes / Servings: 9

Ingredients:
1/3 cup whole wheat Flour
2 tbsps. organic Butter
1 tbsp. Sugar
Water
2 Medium Red Apples, peeled and diced
Pinch of Cinnamon
Pinch of Sugar

Directions:
- Preheat your air fryer to 355F.
- Mix the flour and butter together. Then mix in the sugar. Slowly mix in water a tbsp. at a time until the mixture turns into a dough. Kneads the dough until it's smooth. Then use a rolling pin to roll it out
- Grease ramekins with butter.
- Cover the inside of the ramekin with dough. Then place an equal amount of apples in each ramekin. Top with sugar and cinnamon.
- Put a layer of the dough on top of each ramekin. Use a fork to poke some hole in the dough.
- Place the ramekins in the basket of your preheated air fryer and set the timer for 18 minutes. The banana is cooked when the chocolate melts, the peel turns black, and the banana is soft.
- Allow the pies to cool for a few minutes before serving.

Chocolate M&M Cookies

Chocolate chip cookies are always on the menu. Take time out to try these delicious little tidbits. Your family will enjoy this little treat!

Prep Time: 10 Minutes / Cook Time: 20 Minutes / Servings: 2

Ingredients:
½ cup organic Butter
½ cup Sugar
1 ½ cups Self Raising whole wheat Flour
1 tsp. Vanilla Extract
5 tbsp. skim Milk
3 tbsps. Cocoa
1 bag of M&M's candy
¼ cup White Chocolate

Directions:
- Preheat your air fryer to 355F.
- Put the sugar, cocoa, and flour in a bowl and combine until well mixed. Mix in the butter and then the vanilla.
- Break the white chocolate into small pieces and mix it in along with the milk in the cocoa mixture.
- Knead the dough until it becomes soft.
- Roll out the dough and cut out round cookies.
- Place half of the M&M's in the dough and half of them on top of it.
- Place the cookies in an air fryer safe baking tray.
- Place the dish in the basket of your preheated air fryer and set the timer for 10 minutes.
- Allow the cookies to cool for a few minutes before serving.

Banana Churro

This is a somewhat healthier version of a churro. The banana is coated with breadcrumbs and cinnamon sugar to get the crunchy texture of a churro and a similar flavor. The center is nice and soft and delicious. Feel less guilty about eating a few of them because they're not fried and use a healthy banana instead of dough.

Prep Time: 10 Minutes / Cook Time: 20 Minutes / Servings: 3

Ingredients:
2 Large Bananas
1/2 Cup whole wheat Flour
a pinch of salt
2 organic Eggs, whisked
3/4 Cup panko Bread Crumbs
Cinnamon Sugar, to taste
Olive Oil

Directions:
- Preheat your air fryer to 355.
- Cut each banana into 3 pieces
- Mix the flour and salt together in one bowl, place the eggs in another, the breadcrumbs in a 3rd bowl, and the cinnamon sugar in a 4th.
- Dip the bananas in the flour, then egg, then finally breadcrumbs.
- Place a small amount of olive oil in another bowl and lightly coat the bananas with it.
- Place the bananas in your air fryer in 2 batches and cook for 8 minutes. Shake the basket halfway through.
- Roll the cooked bananas in the cinnamon sugar and serve.

What's Next On The List!

Review Time...

PLEASE LEAVE US AN AMAZON REVIEW!

If you were pleased with our book then leave us a review on Amazon where you purchased this book! **Simply click the link**, scroll to the bottom & review!

>>> Amazon.com/dp/B07F1S5ZZD <<<

In the world of an author who writes books independently, your reviews are not only touching but important so that we know you like the material we have prepared for "you" our audience! So, leave us a review...we would love to see that you enjoyed our book!

If for any reason that you were less than happy with your experience then send me an email at **Info@RecipeNerds.com** and let me know how we can better your experience. We always come out with a few volumes of our books and will possibly be able to address some of your concerns. Do keep in mind that we strive to do our best to give you the highest quality of what "we the independent authors" pour our heart and tears into.

Hello all...I am very excited that you have purchased one of my publications. Please feel free to give us an amazon review where you purchased the book! If you already have, then I thank you for your many great reviews and comments! With a warm heart! ~Alicia Patterson "Personal & Professional Chef"

Sarah Conner

Yours for Looking

"<u>BONUS</u>" Get Your Air Fryer Marinades for Meats & Veggies Now!

Get your very own Air Fryer Marinade Quick Start Guide! This quick start guide will show you how to get the best tasting foods when cooking from your air fryer! **GET YOURS NOW** by just simply clicking the button below! **Enjoy!**

http://eepurl.com/dzsApr

Metric Volume, metric weight and oven temperature charts are tools that everyone wants in the kitchen, but are never around when you need them. That's why we have created these charts for you so you never skip a beat when you're cooking! Hope this helps! :)

Metric Volume Conversions Chart

US Volume Measure	Metric Equivalent
1/8 teaspoon	0.5 milliliters
1/4 teaspoon	1 milliliter
1/2 teaspoon	2.5 milliliters
3/4 teaspoon	4 milliliters
1 teaspoon	5 milliliters
1 1/4 teaspoons	6 milliliters
1 1/2 teaspoons	7.5 milliliters
1 3/4 teaspoons	8.5 milliliters
2 teaspoons	10 milliliters
1/2 tablespoon	7.5 milliliters
1 tablespoon (3 teaspoons, 1/2 fluid ounce)	15 milliliters
2 tablespoons (1 fluid ounce)	30 milliliters
1/4 cup (4 tablespoons)	60 milliliters
1/3 cup	90 milliliters
1/2 cup (4 fluid ounces)	125 milliliters
2/3 cup	160 milliliters
3/4 cup (6 fluid ounces)	180 milliliters
1 cup (16 tablespoons, 8 fluid ounces)	250 milliliters
1 1/4 cups	300 milliliters
1 1/2 cups (12 fluid ounces)	360 milliliters
1 2/3 cups	400 milliliters
2 cups (1 pint)	500 Milliliters
3 cups	700 Milliliters
4 cups (1 quart)	950 milliliters
1 quart plus 1/4 cup	1 liter
4 quarts (1 gallon)	3.8 liters

Metric Weight Conversion Chart

US Weight Measure	Metric Equivalent
1/2 ounce	7 grams
1/2 ounce	15 grams
3/4 ounce	21 grams
1 ounce	28 grams
1 1/4 ounces	35 grams
1 1/2 ounces	42.5 grams
1 2/3 ounces	45 grams
2 ounces	57 grams
3 ounces	85 grams
4 ounces (1/4 pound)	113 grams
5 ounces	142 grams
6 ounces	170 grams
7 ounces	198 grams
8 ounces (1/2 pound)	227 grams
12 ounces (3/4 pound)	340 Grams
16 ounces (1 pound)	454 grams
32.5 ounces (2.2 pounds)	1 kilogram

Temperature Conversion Chart

Degrees Fahrenheit	Degrees Celsius	Cool to Hot
200° F	100° C	Very cool oven
250° F	120° C	Very cool oven
275° F	140° C	Cool oven
300° F	150° C	Cool oven
325° F	160° C	Very moderate oven
350° F	180° C	Moderate oven
375° F	190° C	Moderate oven
400° F	200° C	Moderately hot oven
425° F	220° C	Hot oven
450° F	230° C	Hot oven
475° F	246° C	Very hot oven

About The Author

Sara Conner is a southern girl from the heart of Texas that has made a home for herself in the southern California area. She has worked in the home of several select celebrities for the past 12-15 years. She is a lover of reading and inspiring others to cook like she has taught herself. She also enjoys long romantic walks on the beach and swimming in the ocean. Sarah is always whipping up new recipes for her audience and putting them in her publications!

"Hello and thank you for the purchase! I hope that this book captures your heart and give you more than enough ideas to what you can do with an air fryer! Enjoy!" Sarah Conner, xoxo

Sarah Conner

Air Fryer Creation Recipes & Notes:

Create your very own "Marvelous Masterpieces". Log all of them in this section. You will be amazed on how many ideas you come up with!
Now get creating!

Name	Temp.	Time	Special Toppings or Glaze

CPSIA information can be obtained
at www.ICGtesting.com
Printed in the USA
FSHW011250031019
62657FS